COWARD ON FILM

The Cinema of Noël Coward

Following page: December 14, 1969. Richard Attenborough (left) hosts an evening at London's National Film Theatre devoted to the films of Noël Coward in celebration of his 70th birthday, the beginning of what Noël termed "Holy Week."

COWARD ON FILM

The Cinema of Noël Coward

BARRY DAY

Foreword by
SIR JOHN MILLS

Designed by Bernard Schleifer

The Scarecrow Press, Inc.
Lanham, Maryland • Toronto • Oxford
2005

SCARECROW PRESS, INC.

Published in the United States of America
by Scarecrow Press, Inc.
A wholly owned subsidiary of The Rowman & Littlefield Publishing Group, Inc.
4501 Forbes Boulevard, Suite 200, Lanham, Maryland 20706
www.scarecrowpress.com

PO Box 317
Oxford
OX2 9RU, UK

British Library Cataloguing in Publication Information Available

Library of Congress Cataloging-in-Publication Data

Day, Barry.
    Coward on film : the cinema of Noël Coward / Barry Day ; foreword by
John Mills.
        p. cm.
    Includes bibliographical references and index.
    ISBN 0-8108-5358-2 (alk. paper)
    1. Coward, Noël, 1899–1973—Film and video adaptations. 2. Film adaptations.
I. Title.
    PR6005.O85Z6235 2004
    791.43'6—dc22   2004058929

To Graham Payn

(not forgetting Tim Verney
and Mr. Keats . . .)

Coward on Film

vii

C O N T E N T S

FOREWORD

I HAVE ALWAYS CONSIDERED MYSELF a very lucky man, but the biggest stroke of luck I ever had was to meet Noël Coward in Singapore. I had been on tour in the Far East with a company which went under the illustrious name of "The Quaints," who did thirty plays, musicals and Shakespeare. I turned up in Singapore one night after a day's traveling, hot and tired, and was told by our advance manager that Noël Coward was in front. I said—"Oh good, so's God," but he actually *was.*

What had happened was that he was traveling back from New York where he had produced *Bitter Sweet.* His traveling companion, Earl Amherst, was taken ill and Noël was forced to stay in Singapore. The theatre always drew him like a magnet and he found a rickshaw to go in search of the Theatre Royal, which had over its entrance an advertisement saying "Tonight: The Quaints in *Hamlet.*" More luck. We were supposed to be playing *Hamlet* in which I appeared as the 2nd Gravedigger doubling with Osric, but Horatio got drunk at the governor's cocktail party and we had to switch quickly to the Vivian Ellis musical *Mr. Cinders,* in which I played a star part, a wonderful chance to show off with five numbers and a tap dance. Noël came backstage and that was how it happened.

When I got back to London six months later he arranged an audition at His Majesty's Theatre in front of Sir Charles Blake Cochran and I opened at the Opera House, Manchester, in Cochran's revue (*Words and Music*) one month later.

I worked with Noel many times after that on stage and screen and it was always a wonderful experience. I particularly remember *In Which We Serve,* in which Noël played the lead, and it was directed by a then unknown David Lean. Noël brought the discipline of the theatre into the film studio and the film was an enormous hit.

I wish this book a great success.

—SIR JOHN MILLS

ACKNOWLEDGMENTS

I WOULD LIKE TO THANK the following for their help in preparing this book. You all know what you did. . . .

British Film Institute (BFI) staff in London
Alan Brodie (AB Representation)
Rosalind Fayne
Geoffrey Johnson
Larry Kardish and Josh Siegel
(Film & Video Department at the Museum of Modern Art)
Howard Mandelbaum (Photofest)
Sir John Mills
Stephen Ryan (Scarecrow Press)
Bernard Schleifer
Ron Simon (Museum of TV & Radio)
Christopher Sinclair-Stevenson and the Alec Guinness Estate
Peter Tummons (Methuen)

INTRODUCTION

> I'm not very keen on Hollywood . . . I'd rather
> have a nice cup of cocoa, really.
>
> —NOËL COWARD in a letter to his mother c.1930

ACTRESS MARIE TEMPEST ONCE EXPRESSED WHAT SEEMED TO BE A SELF-
contradictory opinion of Noël Coward when she said, "I do not think he will
ever quite fulfill his promise if he does not curb his versatility."

Since Miss Tempest died in 1942, she was almost certainly referring to
Coward the actor-playwright-lyricist-composer and all-around celebrity. At
that point he had experienced no more than two flirtations with film; in neither of which was he in a position to exert any personal creative control.
Nonetheless, her remark showed extreme prescience, as far as his subsequent
career was concerned. Looked at retrospectively, the report card would
read—"Undoubted ability with flashes of brilliance. If only he would concentrate, he would certainly excel."

Like Gaul, *Coward on Film* falls roughly into three parts. The late 1920s
to the outbreak of World War II was mainly devoted to watching other
people adapting the theatrical work for the screen with varying degrees of
success. The 1940s was the golden period in which he took enough of an
active interest in the process to involve himself personally as producer, writer
and—occasionally—as performer. Finally, from the late 1950s to the late
'60s, we have Noël Coward, actor for hire, emerging intermittently from one
or other of his retreats to steal someone else's picture.

That much the world saw. Only in his *Diaries* does one get the occasional
sense that he might like to have tried his hand at more, if only the demons
of boredom with the *process* of filmmaking could have been tamed or—more
to the point—if he could have realised sooner the futility of insisting on pre-
war Coward in a post-war world. Once he came to reluctant terms with the
new realities and discovered other talents within himself, he found a new
lease on creative life in TV, cabaret and film and late resurgence of his theatrical reputation in what he gleefully termed "Dad's Renaissance." But by

then too much of the time he might have profitably employed in new directions—such as film—had been wasted.

   We must be grateful for what we have been left. As is so often the case
with Coward, he managed to achieve more with what he put part of his mind
to than most people do in a full-time career.

*   *   *   *

In retrospect it's easy enough to see what happened. Noël's youthful precoc-
ity with both words and music were so quickly rewarded by performance and
acclaim that the stumbling, finally stuttering, infant medium of cinema must
have seemed a creative *cul-de-sac* to someone so verbally oriented. What
other people did to his early plays can hardly have reassured him. The
movies, certainly in England, were a blunt instrument; he was not going to
enhance his reputation *that* way.

   At the time of the filming of his early plays he gave an interview to the fan
magazine *The Picturegoer* (August 1927) in which he said, among other things . . .

> The screen's limitations? Too much is talked about them . . . All art has limita-
> tions, but as they are found in all forms of expression, why grumble at films in
> particular? You lose the actor's voice on the screen. But then you don't hear the
> voice of a character in a novel, either.
>
>   No, films are not an off-shoot of the stage. They are a totally different
> medium . . .

He did agree that film drama—like stage drama—should have "constructive
form and the minimum of digression." Even so, he did not feel he wanted to
give his full attention to writing for the screen.

> You may take it that I am not interested in writing scenarios at all. I want to write
> words, not stage directions. I don't want to cast any slur on scenario work, and I
> readily admit that it is a highly expert business. But as a dramatist, dialogue and its
> psychology are practically my sole concern. You will notice that in the published
> version of my plays the stage directions are cut down to the absolute minimum . . .
> it is work which simply does not appeal to me.

In summing up he evoked the critic who had recently remarked that
"Coward doth make consciences of us all":

> Let British producers be honest with themselves and do their best without ref-
> erence to what the public are wrongly supposed to demand. Let us hear less
> about "film mentality" and "we must put that in for the box-office." Pandering
> is a mistake—especially when it is not based on facts.

At the time of the interview he was actively working on his first original sce-
nario—*Concerto*—which was eventually rejected, almost certainly reinforcing
his lack of enthusiasm for the *parvenu* form.

Nonetheless, the phenomenon of actually *making* films fascinated him just as much as any other aspect of the human comedy. Hollywood—when he first visited it in the early 1930s—he found as bizarre as any of its output. In *Past Conditional* he wrote:

So much has been written about Hollywood both in praise and dispraise that I feel it would be redundant to add my own views to the swollen flood; however, I cannot resist making a few comments . . . For those readers of movie magazines who imagine that life in that unique Never Never Land is an endless round of glamorous parties and star-spangled orgies, the truth would be sadly disillusioning. Perhaps in its earlier years when fascinating silent stars galloped about on mettlesome horses, indulged in over-publicised marriages and divorces and flung themselves in and out of each other's swimming pools life was less real and less earnest. Now, at any rate it is so controlled and ordered as to be almost humdrum. True, on Saturday nights with a work-free Sabbath just ahead, there are occasional social and even sexual junketings, but on the other six evenings of the week most of the big box office stars are usually in bed by ten with Ovaltine rather than Champagne and scripts rather than lovers. Film-making, contrary to much popular belief, is a demanding and exhausting business. The working hours alone preclude many opportunities for casual dalliance. During the shooting period of any movie not only the floor crews and the studio operators but the directors and extras and actors have to be ready and on the set by eight o'clock in the morning. For those performers who happen to be playing characters necessitating an elaborate makeup, the call is still earlier. This, taking into account the time getting to the studio from wherever you happen to be living, means being torn from sleep at about five-thirty A.M. When I was making my first picture *The Scoundrel* in 1935 at the Paramount Astoria Studios in Brooklyn, I remember driving over the 59th Street Bridge every morning for weeks and watching the dawn come up. In Hollywood, of course, owing to the climate for one thing, conditions are more agreeable than in New York in mid-winter. To watch the sun rise over majestic mountains and the Pacific Ocean is pleasanter than watching it rise over skyscrapers and blocks of dirty ice drifting down the East River.

Another dismaying facet of "Movie" life in Hollywood—and alas elsewhere—is the soul-destroying tradition of "conferences." I don't know when this ghastly innovation first came into being but I do know from personal experience that it is the most monumental, ego-strutting time-waster in the business. A film conference, ideally speaking, should be a brief discussion between the director and heads of departments concerning ways and means, general procedure and time schedules. What it usually is is nothing of the sort. A large group of people, many of them redundant, sits around a table in somebody's office with pads and pencils and sometimes a jug of water and a few glasses in front of them, and talks a great deal . . .

The first film conference I ever attended took place in Hollywood three days after I had landed from my South American travels, in an office on the Fox lot. As I entered the room my heart sank at the familiar spectacle. There was the shiny table, there were the pads and pencils and the jugs of water. On this occasion, however, it was not Child Welfare that was to be discussed but the movie version of *Cavalcade*. Also present was a collection of people, many of whom I had never seen before and have never seen since. What their particular functions were and why they were present I had as little idea then as I have now. In due course, after various introductions had been made, we all sat down. I was placed on the right of the Chairman whose name unfortunately eludes me. He was exceedingly courteous and had one of those affable grey faces that one immediately forgets. An anonymous script writer—not Reginald Berkely, who ultimately did a fine script—was invited by the Chairman to start the ball rolling by giving us his ideas. There was a slight pause while he put on his glasses and assembled a sheaf of typewritten sheets of paper before him. He then cleared his throat and began, with admirable assurance, to speak.

"The opening of the picture as I see it should be as follows." He paused, consulted his notes for a moment and then went on. "After the credits, which should rise slowly up the screen from the bottom to the top against a panorama of moving clouds, we see the branch of a tree in winter. The branch is flecked with snow, and on it is perched a little bird, just one little bird, looking lonely and forlorn. As we look at the little bird the background music swells and it is suddenly Spring. The tree is covered with tender young leaves and the original bird has been joined by hundreds of other birds, fluttering and chirrupping and building their nests." He sat back in his chair and regarded us with a complacent smile. Whether he expected us to give a round of applause or cry in unison that we did believe in fairies I shall never know because, seized with a violent inward fury, I rose to my feet. I think it was that smile as much as anything else that exasperated me. I looked around the table at all those vacuous faces waiting attentively for further treacly symbolism and realised with dreadful clarity that all the worst stories I had heard about the Hollywood mentality must have been, if anything, understated. I also knew that if I stayed at that table one minute longer I should probably lose my temper and be very rude indeed and that to make an ugly scene at such an early stage of the proceedings would do more harm than good. So, forcing my lips into an apologetic smile, I said that I had completely forgotten an appointment of pressing urgency at the Beverly Wilshire Hotel and left the conference room, never to return.

Which explains why in a letter to his mother written about this time Noël could write—"I'm not very keen on Hollywood . . . I'd rather have a nice cup of cocoa, really."

Over the years there were to be many trips to Hollywood and many friends to be made there.

Over time, though, the place began to pall. As early as the 1930s he would complain that people in the film industry "work too deuced hard. They get up at 6:30 . . . stand around all day under the red-hot lights . . . eat hurriedly at mid-day, and because they are too tired to sit up late at night have their supper served on trays. That's no way to live, and certainly no way to work." And as for being a writer: "How they accomplish anything in the rabbit hutches to which they are assigned is beyond me. They even punch time clocks."

During a fleeting 1948 visit—to discuss making a film version of *Long Island Sound* with George Cukor—his feelings were reconfirmed: "I suddenly realised something and that was that I would not do a picture in Hollywood

. . . There is something about the atmosphere here that is utterly defeating. I don't think I could bear it for longer than a brief visit. . . . There is certainly too much movie mentality about and it is all far too big."

His description of a not-so-marvellous Hollywood party on that same visit says it all: "It was a nice party, except for Joan Fontaine's titties which kept falling about, and a large rock python which was handed to me as a surprise."

After his Las Vegas cabaret success in 1955 there was an avalanche of offers. "Paramount want me to do a picture with Danny Kaye and *The Sleeping Prince* and/or anything I bloody well like on my own terms. M-G-M want me to play the Prince in *The Swan*. Twentieth Century-Fox are sitting with their fingers crossed."

There is no evidence that he ever took any of the overtures seriously. Olivier eventually made *The Sleeping Prince* with Marilyn Monroe as *The Prince and the Showgirl* (1957), and Alec Guinness made *The Swan* (1956) with Grace Kelly. In fact, the only time Noël ever went to work there was not on a film at all but to make the TV version of *Blithe Spirit* in 1956.

His single American studio experience as an actor was in New York in 1935—at which time he told an interviewer he found the working atmosphere "sprawling, untidy and wasteful."

* * * *

Even when sound came in and provided an opportunity for the Coward dialogue to be heard, the filmmakers felt they knew better what cinema audiences wanted. *Private Lives* survived relatively intact but *Design for Living* did not. Even a screenwriter as literate as Ben Hecht could boast that "only one word of original Coward" survived the transition from play script to screen. It was hardly surprising that Noël refused to be disabused of his early prejudices. He took the money and ran back to the safety of the West End stage.

And the money on offer could indeed be substantial. One offer he did not take—from Fox—was £600,000 for the rights to *Cavalcade, Bitter Sweet* and *Hay Fever*. In the event Fox only made *Cavalcade*. *Bitter Sweet* was left to the tender mercies of M-G-M—and *Hay Fever* has yet to be filmed.

His verdict on Hollywood at the time: "I don't want to be rich—I want to be happy . . ."

It was the war that changed this like so many things. Noël was anxious to serve his country in some significant way and was mortified when Churchill told him that he could best be employed entertaining the troops. Yes, of course he would entertain the troops—and did so several thousand times—but he wanted to do more. If he couldn't get in the front line in some way, no one could stop him from doing what Noël Coward did best—write.

He determined to write the definitive *song* for the times—just as Ivor Novello had done in World War I with "Keep the Home Fires Burning." He wrote "London Pride." A *play*? He wrote several between 1939 and 1941 but it was *Blithe Spirit* that distracted Britons from the bombs for the duration of the conflict. And then they asked him to make a *film*. Two independent producers gave him carte blanche to write and act in anything of his choosing and the very next day his friend Lord Louis Mountbatten described the sinking of his own ship and the heroism of the men in it. The coincidence seemed providential and Noël's film career began again in earnest with *In Which We Serve*.

The close relationship that developed between Noël, producer Anthony Havelock-Allan, director David Lean and cameraman Ronald Neame was to lead to three further collaborations on Coward material over the next four years, but it was the last of these, *Brief Encounter*, that pulled all the creative threads together in a film that compressed the greatest of emotions into a perfect English miniature.

Brief Encounter was the high water mark of Coward the film author, but if he had done nothing more than that and *In Which We Serve*, he would have two of the most definitive genre films ever made in Britain to his credit.

Both of them depended on the inspired and intuitive collaboration of complementary talents. Realising that and finding them missing from his next two projects, Noël retired from making films and occupied the rest of his active life with appearing in them.

* * * *

By this time he was in his mid-fifties, a little "long in the tooth" (as he would have put it) for leading roles. And to be honest, it's more than likely that the theatricality of "Noël Coward" the persona would always have been more suited to stage than screen. Larger than life personalities have always had trouble submerging themselves, no matter how considerable their technique. His friend Orson Welles had the same trouble for most of his career. The public reaction was always likely to be: "Oh, look . . . there's Orson (or Noël) being . . ."

By the time he came to it, Noël was clever enough to make that the *point* of his performances. There was always the implied wink at the audience, the suggestion of "Well, *this* is a bit of fun, isn't it?" When the material happened to fit the approach, the result was riveting. The part of Hawthorne, the educated public school idiot from M.1.5 in *Our Man in Havana* showed the art of the possible. The sight of Noël, pin stripe suited, homburg hatted and with regulation umbrella furled, striding though the seedy streets of Graham Greene's Havana as though they were St. James's was one to treasure. Later the character of Mr. Bridger, the incarcerated crime lord, pulling the strings of "the Italian job" from a prison cell decorated with photos of the Royal Family, made one wonder who else could have played the part.

It was to be his last as well as one of his best parts. Symbolically, the last we see of Mr. Bridger is of him receiving the ovation of his fellow inmates for pulling off the "job." Hands raised to accept what, after all, he knew to be his due, it seems now like a fitting and prophetic image of the actor taking his own farewell.

PART ONE

Based on a Play by Noël Coward . . .

Coward
on Film

1

In the silent version of The Queen Was in the Parlour (1927)—*retitled* Forbidden Love *for the U.S. market—Lili Damita played the part of Nadya with what Noël considered "excessive vivacity."*

THE SILENT PERIOD

The name of Michael Balcon is now firmly linked with that of Ealing Studios and the golden age of British post-war film comedy. What is less well documented is his earlier incarnation at Gainsborough Pictures, starting in 1924, the latter part of the silent era. In an attempt to compete with Hollywood "product," he adopted one of their proven techniques—to adapt material already popular with the public in some other medium. The novel was an obvious source but, increasingly, so was the stage play. Consequently, at the end of the 1920s, Balcon quickly snapped up a number of theatrical hits by the likes of Ivor Novello, Margaret Kennedy and—Noël Coward.

For the young Coward the timing couldn't have been more opportune. The *succès de scandale* represented by *The Vortex* (1924) had made him the most talked about and controversial playwright since Shaw and Maugham, nor was he at all averse to being turned into a media celebrity. Balcon bought up three of his early plays and filmed all of them in 1927 for release in early 1928. In keeping with another Hollywood tradition, the author had precious little control over what happened to his work.

THE QUEEN WAS IN THE PARLOUR (1927)

The original play was written in 1922 and first produced in 1926, when it had a run of 136 performances.

PLAY SYNOPSIS

Nadya, the young widow of Archduke Alexander of Krayia, is now living in Paris, where she has met and fallen in love with Sabien Pastal. Returning from yet another party, they debate their future. Nadya admits she would like to go back to her country some day, but her life is now here with Sabien. They decide to get married right away.

Soon after Sabien has left, Nadya receives a visit from General Krish, bringing the news that her father has been assassinated. She is now Queen and must return to Krayia immediately. Nadya tries everything in her power to avoid her destiny but finally she is forced to agree to leave Paris on the next train. She barely has time to write Sabien a farewell note.

A year later and we are in the royal palace, where Queen Nadya receives Prince Keri, whom she is to marry the following day. Outside there is the sound of gunfire. Revolution is in the air. A would-be assassin has just tried to shoot the Queen but been stopped by a man in the crowd. Nadya and Keri meet in private for the first time since their marriage has been "arranged" and discover that each of them has been obliged to give up their true love for the sake of duty.

General Krish suggests she may like to thank her unknown saviour in person and brings in "M. Florent," who turns out to be none other than a distraught Sabien. She pleads with him to go away and claims she no longer loves him but neither can keep up the pretence for long. They cannot change Fate but she agrees to spend this one last night with him.

Later that evening Sabien arrives to wait for Nadya's return from a state dinner. She is accompanied by Keri and it is clear they have reached an understanding. Theirs will be a marriage of friends. Keri takes his leave and Nadya joins Sabien in the inner room, where they talk gaily, almost hysterically, of old times. Slowly the conversation dies away and they look at one another in silence.

It is four in the morning. In the Queen's antechamber Krish and Keri are keeping watch, awaiting the news that the revolution has begun. Suddenly the lights go out. The telephone rings and then falls silent. The moment has come. They rush to wake Nadya, who now appears, closing her bedroom door carefully behind her. She flatly refuses to take their advice and flee the country.

Outside the noise of the crowd grows louder and a stone is thrown through the window. For Nadya this is the breaking point. She rushes out on to the balcony and shouts at the crowd to shoot her, if they have the courage. She is joined by Keri, who suggest that everyone needs a good night's sleep. The crowd finds this amusing, laughs and disperses.

At that moment they hear a shot from the bedroom. Krish enters to announce that a strange man has been shot trying to enter the Queen's bedroom. Nadya knows differently. Sabien, unable to face the prospect of life without her, has shot himself. Only Keri guesses at the truth.

* * * *

The film version was made by Gainsborough Pictures in 1927. It was first shown at the Avenue Pavilion cinema in February 1928.

CREDITS

Producer	Michael Balcon
Director	Graham Cutts
Screen Adaptation	Graham Cutts

CAST

Nadya	Lili Damita
Sabien	Paul Richter
Prince Keri	Harry Leichke
Zana	Rosa Richards
General Krish	Klein Rogge
The Grand Duchess Emilie of Zalgar	Trude Hesterberg

* * * *

The play, Coward admitted later, "was my one and only expedition into Ruritania and I enjoyed it very much . . . Anthony Hope had blazed the trail, and what was good enough for Anthony Hope was good enough for me." He was also honest enough to speculate that the play "will be old-fashioned long before *The Prisoner of Zenda* and *Rupert of Hentzau*." In that he was undoubtedly right, although the piece had enough of a shelf life to be remade only five years later in a sound version—*Tonight Is Ours* (1932).

The film was adapted and directed in a reasonably faithful but pedestrian fashion by contract director Graham Cutts. The palace and party sets are lavish and—unusually for British films of the period—there is extensive location shooting in Paris and an unnamed ski resort. Only one shot surprises and disturbs the even tenor of the piece. When the would be assassin threatens Nadya, we find ourselves looking at her down the barrel of the gun, very much as—thirty years later—we shall do in the James Bond title sequence. Knowing that Alfred Hitchcock was Cutts's assistant director at this time, is it reading too much into a few frames of film to identify "the Hitchcock touch" in embryo? *The Queen* cut little box office ice, not because audiences were tired of day trips to Ruritania but because the piece—originally written and produced on stage in 1922—was no longer what was expected of "that clever young Mr. Coward" by the time it reached the screen.

Noël himself considered it was "played with excessive vivacity by Lili Damita."

EASY VIRTUE (1927)

Easy Virtue was written in 1924 and first produced in the United States in 1925, then in London in 1926, where it had a run of 124 performances.

PLAY SYNOPSIS

The action takes place in the country house of Colonel and Mrs. Whittaker, where they live with their two daughters, Marion—a somewhat religious young woman—and Hilda, who is still at school. They receive a telegram from their son, John, to say that he is arriving with his newly-married wife, Larita. This is a bolt from the blue to all of them. Mrs. Whittaker is particularly disconcerted, because she has invited Sarah—the girl John was supposed to marry—to lunch. Sarah, however, doesn't seem particularly upset. She asks if she can bring a friend, Charles, with her.

John and Larita arrive. She is a beautiful, elegant woman and not at all what the family had expected. Consternation ensues when it transpires that she is not only older than John but also a divorcée.

Three months later and the strains are beginning to show. Larita is bored with the life the Whittakers lead and they—with the exception of the colonel—have all determined to freeze her out. She confides to the colonel that even the marriage is going wrong. Ironically, her only friend is Sarah.

During the preparations for the annual dance the Whittakers always host, a series of confrontations occur in which the Whittaker women express their hostility towards Larita and she defends herself creditably. The culmination of these incidents is that Mrs. Whittaker asks Larita to remain in her room during the dance.

The dance is in full swing. All the main characters and their various friends and partners mingle. Mrs. Whittaker is busily explaining that her daughter-in-law is indisposed with a headache, when Larita appears, dressed to the nines. She proceeds to deal with all of them so that they are totally nonplussed. In a quiet moment she admits to Charles—with whom she has established a rapport—that she now realises that marrying John was the most cowardly thing she ever did—"He falls short of every ideal I ever had."

She later confides to Sarah that she intends to leave that night for good, asking Sarah to look after John—her way of saying that she hopes the two of them will now make a match of it. The man servant arrives to tell her the car is waiting. With a last sad look around the garden and with the sounds of the party in her ears, she walks out.

* * * *

The film version was made by Gainsborough Pictures in 1927. It was first shown at the Stoll Cinema in March 1928.

CREDITS

Producers	Michael Balcon and C. M. Woolf
Director	Alfred Hitchcock
Screen Adaptation	Alfred Hitchcock and Eliot Stannard
Director of Photography	Claude McDonell
Editor	Ivor Montagu

CAST

Larita Fitton	Isabel Jeans
Her Husband	Franklyn Dyall
The Co-Respondent	Eric Bransby-Williams
Plaintiff's Counsel	Ian Hunter
John Whittaker	Robert Irvine
His Mother (Mrs. Whittaker)	Violet Farebrother
His Father (Colonel Whittaker)	Frank Elliot
His Elder Sister (Marion)	Dacia Deane
His Younger Sister (Hilda)	Dorothy Boyd
Sarah (Hurst)	Enid Stamp-Taylor
With: Benita Hume	

* * * *

With *Easy Virtue* Balcon assigned one of his contract directors, Alfred Hitchcock, for what was to be his fifth film and his fifth collaboration with screenplay writer Eliot Stannard. By all accounts, it was not a subject that Hitchcock found particularly challenging. Only the previous year he had made the acclaimed *The Lodger*, a version of the Jack the Ripper legend that foreshadowed the kind of film on which he was to build his reputation. By comparison this mannered study of social manners and *mores* lacked the "edge" he was looking for and he made his lack of enthusiasm clear to Balcon.

Nonetheless, once the film was under way, he contrived to put his stamp on it. The drama that Hitchcock saw in the material was the heroine's ostracism and betrayal by her in-laws, a process aggravated by the attention of the press on the scent of a scandal—a prescient touch, seen from a perspective of seventy years later! Balcon was sceptical of this change of emphasis, which removed any lingering element of the comedy of manners Noël had intended, but allowed the director to have his way. Whether he blamed Hitchcock for the film's subsequent failure at the box office is not recorded.

The whole first section of the film consists of the director's composing the storyline he felt Noël *should* have written. There is a lengthy opening trial scene at the end of which Larita is condemned by the jury for her moral transgressions. She then tries to live incognito on the Riviera but is recognized wherever she goes as the "notorious Mrs. Fitton." Eventually, she meets the impressionable John Whittaker, who marries her, and the story proper is allowed to begin.

Seen today, *Easy Virtue* holds the interest mainly for one or two early signs of "the Hitchcock touch." However unsympathetic he found the basic material, he instinctively found ways to dramatise the action. Typical of the later Hitchcock is the scene where the judge surveys the leading characters in his court room. Using his monocle he literally brings them into focus one by one. The scene ends with a dissolve from the swinging monocle to the pendulum of a clock.

Right: The Master confers with the Master of Suspense (Alfred Hitchcock). Their professional paths crossed only once. In 1927 Hitch directed a silent version of Easy Virtue *and virtually rewrote the plot! Below: Larita (Isabel Jeans) and John (Franklyn Dyall).*

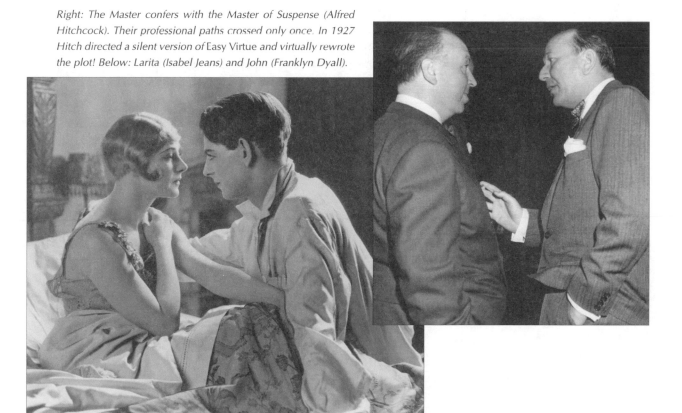

When the couple moves from France to London, Hitchcock uses the symbolism of dogs. A French poodle turns into a British bulldog.

The passing of time becomes a theme in the film. Years later—in a conversation with fellow director François Truffaut—Hitchcock became almost enthusiastic about one particular scene:

> When John is proposing marriage to Larita, instead of giving him an immediate answer, she says—"I'll call you from my house, around midnight." Next, we show a little watch, indicating it is midnight; it's the watch of a switchboard operator who is reading a book. A small light goes on the board. She puts the plug in and is about to go back to her reading but automatically listens in to the earphones. Then, she puts the book down, obviously fascinated by the phone conversation. In other words, I never show either of the two people. You follow what is happening by watching the switchboard operator.

After a lap dissolve of some forty years Hitchcock's memory may be allowed some leeway. In point of fact, Larita says that she will phone with her answer "some time this evening"; we find the telephone operator in mid shot and never see her watch in close-up. What he might have added is that the next shot is a close-up of a luggage label with the words "Mrs. John Whittaker." The operator was played by the unknown and uncredited Benita Hume, who was given star status in her next film.

By way of contrast, he also recollected the film contained "the worst title I've ever written." After her divorce, Larita leaves the court and is hounded by the 1920s equivalent of the paparazzi. "She appears at the courthouse stairs, her arms out, and says—'Shoot, there's nothing left to kill!'"

Hitchcock's enthusiasm for the occasional visual touches he was able to bring to the story underlines not merely his instinctive approach to telling stories on film by emphasising the significant detail but the crucial problem of translating Coward's articulate—and at this stage often melodramatic—plays into an essentially nonverbal medium. Even if Noël had been invited to write his own "titles," he could not have captured the cut and thrust of the kind of stage dialogue he was beginning to perfect.

THE VORTEX (1927)

The play was written in 1923, first produced at the Everyman Theatre, Hampstead, in 1924 and subsequently transferred. There were 236 performances.

PLAY SYNOPSIS

The play opens in the Lancasters' flat. A group of her friends gossip about Florence Lancaster's affair with Tom, a younger man the same age as her son,

Nicky. When Florence herself enters, one of the friends, Helen, warns her that Tom is not as much in love with her as she is with him, and that she is making herself look foolish by trying to hold on to her youth in this way.

To everyone's surprise, Nicky enters from Paris, where he has been studying music. He looks thin and far from well and is anything but pleased to hear that his mother won't break her date with Tom to spend time with him. Florence is also upset to hear that Nicky is engaged to Bunty Mainwaring but appears to warm to the girl when she arrives and invites her to her country house party the following weekend.

The house party is in full swing. Nicky turns off the gramophone and sits at the piano to play for the dancers. Looking for a light for her cigarette, Helen goes to Nicky's jacket. He snatches it away angrily but not before she has seen the contents and realised that he is taking drugs.

Florence and Tom argue. She is upset when he gives the reason for being unable to see her: he is going out with his mother. She later proceeds to argue with Nicky, criticising Bunty before leaving. Helen now seeks out Nicky and warns him of the dangers of his drug habit. Later in the evening Bunty breaks off their engagement.

When the others have supposedly gone to bed, Bunty and Tom are left alone. Comparing notes, they find they have much in common and are mutually attracted. Florence and Nicky enter to find them in each other's arms. In an angry scene Florence orders them both from her house. When Tom begins to go, however, she runs after him, throwing her dignity to the winds. Through all of it Nicky plays the piano violently.

Florence takes to her bed. Helen, her one true friend, tries to tell her that Tom and Bunty are obviously right for each other. Florence had better start to literally act her age and face the facts. At which point Nicky bursts in and asks Helen to leave. He needs to talk to his mother in private. Left alone, he demands to know if Tom has been her lover and forces her to own up to the pattern of her life. He accuses her of demeaning his father and ruining his own life with her selfishness and vanity. In turn, he admits his own drug habit. Mother and son are left together, as the curtain falls, each promising to help the other find a better way of life. It is hard to believe they have any real chance of success.

* * * *

The film version was produced by Gainsborough Pictures in 1927 and first shown at the Marble Arch Pavilion in March 1928.

CREDITS

Producer	Michael Balcon
Director	Adrian Brunel
Screenplay	Eliot Stannard
Titles	Roland Pertwee
Photography	James Wilson
Art Director	Clifford Pember

CAST

Nicky Lancaster	Ivor Novello
Florence Lancaster	Willette Kershaw
Bunty Mainwaring	Frances Dobbs
Tom Veryan	Allan Hollis
Pauncefort Quentin	Kinsey Peile
David Lancaster	Sir Simeon Stuart
Anna Volloff	Julie Suedo
Helen Saville	Dorothy Fane

*   *   *   *

When it came to the film version, Balcon was well aware that he faced even greater problems of censorship and sent a representative to consult the British Board of Film Censors. His emissary duly returned with the good news that the property was approved—the only caveats being that the mother must not have a lover and, of course, Nicky could not take drugs!

The rewritten script almost gave Coward apoplexy; it had little or nothing to do with the play he'd written. "When Noël read (it)," Brunel recalled, "he was speechless for a moment and then let out a torrent of criticism that even the telephone couldn't stop." A second version was prepared, which he grudgingly accepted.

Nicky was now played by Ivor Novello, while Lilian Braithwaite's part (Florence) was taken by American stage actress Willette Kershaw. It would be many years before actors who created roles on stage were even considered for the screen version. Noël apparently took a screen test for the part but Novello was a bankable star by this time.

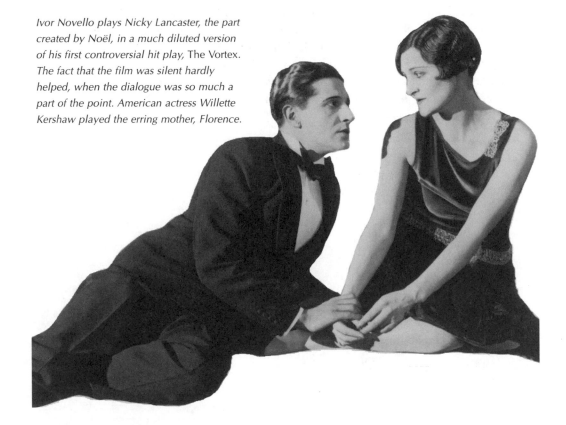

Ivor Novello plays Nicky Lancaster, the part created by Noël, in a much diluted version of his first controversial hit play, The Vortex. The fact that the film was silent hardly helped, when the dialogue was so much a part of the point. American actress Willette Kershaw played the erring mother, Florence.

In point of fact, the play fared better in the translation than might have been expected. The main plot differences are that, while Florence makes it plain from her behaviour what her relationship with Tom is, she never actually *says* that he is her lover, while Nicky only *threatens* to take drugs.

Inevitably, there were certain embellishments to "open up" the stage drama. Nicky no longer returns from Paris but lives in a London flat. He has a painter as a neighbour whose model is a dancer. The girl uses Nicky's music in a revue, and a sequence was shot in which Ivor is seen conducting in the orchestra pit. The scene was not used in the final version, along with another scene in which Nicky and Florence attend a fashion show.

The discovery of drugs ("a little box of forgetfulness") was also restaged. They now belong to the model who is, of course, French (with all that that implies) and were confiscated by Nicky to save her from her fate. Another change was to the ending of the piece. Bunty, having been ordered out of the house when she is discovered with Tom, is asked to stay on by the reconciled Florence and Nicky and the film ends with the three of them embracing in mutual forgiveness.

While the changes sound relatively small, given the intractability of the material, one can understand Noël's apprehension of the cumulative impact. The depth of Nicky's character and thus its tragic potential is undermined. Not only is he *not* running off the rails in Paris, but he is living a relatively conventional life in London, his drug taking exchanged for cocktail shaking and his greatest sin an excess of piano playing. Nor is Bunty the archetypal goodtime girl but a working girl journalist who comes to interview Nicky. Finally, in the climactic bedroom scene it proved difficult to do much significant soul baring with no adultery or drug taking to admit to.

The film's main problem, however, had little to do with any of this. It was simply that much of the play's original impact was not merely the shocking content but the quality of Noël's dialogue. And nothing could make up for the lack of that. Film historian Rachel Low pinned it down when she observed that "epigrams depending on a throwaway delivery looked merely facetious in the portentous pause of a title."

Director Adrian Brunel was understandably nervous about the whole project for just these reasons.

> When I realised the difficulties I had before me in putting over my emasculated *Vortex*, I decided to borrow some of Hitchcock's tactics. It was too late in the day to reconstruct the whole script, but there was much that could still be done to embellish what I had, with a display of technical devices which might divert the critics . . . It was just an extra coating of sugar for the doughnut—to make up for the lack of jam at its centre. These desperate measures were welcomed by my unit and Ivor Novello composed a joyous slogan, with musical accompaniment:

> *A cute shot a day*
> *Keeps the critics at bay.*

Editor Ivor Montagu ironically summed up the filtering process: "Noël Coward's plot: 'Mother, will you give up lovers if I give up drugs?' of necessity became: 'Mummy, will you give up going to teas and dances if I give up ciga-rettes and Aspirins?'"

The critics, by and large, approved of what Brunel had done. *Kine Weekly* decided that although "Noël Coward's play has been filtered . . . considering the difficulties of the story, which is hardly suitable for screen purposes, Adrian Brunel has done very well." *The Bioscope* picked up on the main concern, however, that "Excellent as this production is in many details, it is another proof that the most successful of stage plays is not necessarily a fit subject for the screen."

* * * *

Looking back on the Gainsborough experience years later, Michael Balcon reflected: "We followed trends and did not try to make them. It was doubly a mistake to lean on stage plays because we were making silent films . . . both *(Vortex* and *Easy Virtue)* were financial failures."

There was to be a postscript to the Balcon/Gainsborough/Coward relationship. If it had proved nothing else, it had demonstrated the relative intractability of the original plays for screen adaptation. As a result, Balcon asked Coward to write an original film treatment. The result was a period story called *Concerto* (1928), written with Novello in mind. Balcon found that the script "cried out for music," but he had already contracted to pay Noël the not inconsiderable sum of £1,200 for the property. Perhaps sensing Balcon's instincts were correct, Noël did not argue when it was suggested that the project be called off. In fact, his voluntary decision to return his fee was one of the best he ever made, since he was able to use the basic story line a year later in a medium which did not suffer from the same restrictions. He gave it music and turned it into *Bitter Sweet.*

It may have been his exposure to the kind of rejection all writers of screenplays have to learn to accept that explains the tone of his subsequent reply to a *Picturegoer* interviewer: "You may take it that I am not interested in writing scenarios at all. I want to write words, not stage directions . . . As a dramatist, dialogue and its psychology are practically my whole career."

To another American interviewer he added: "So many (movies) sound as if the speaker's palate had been cut."

It would be more than a decade later before the circumstances came together to create the right conditions for that second attempt.

"SOUND RUNNING . . ."

Of all my plays only one, *Cavalcade* had been filmed with taste and integrity. The rest, with the possible exception of *Private Lives*, which was passable, had been re-written by incompetent hacks, vulgarised by incompetent directors and reduced to common fatuity.

—*Future Indefinite*

PRIVATE LIVES (1931)

The play was written in 1929 and produced in 1930. It opened London's new Phoenix Theatre, where it had a run of 101 performances before transferring to Broadway for a further 248 performances. Noël appeared as Elyot Chase and Gertrude Lawrence as Amanda, with Laurence Olivier as Victor Prynne and Adrianne Allen as Sybil (London) being replaced by Jill Esmond (New York).

PLAY SYNOPSIS

Elyot and Amanda are two people who can't live without each other but experience considerable difficulty living with each other. Divorced two years ago, each has remarried and now—by the coincidence allowed to the dramatist —find themselves on their second honeymoons staying at the same French hotel where they had spent their own. While their respective new partners are dressing for dinner, they encounter one another on their adjacent balconies. Their stilted conversation of reminiscence soon breaks down and they are forced to admit that they are still in love. The new marriages are a sham. Ever impulsive, they run away together, leaving notes for their respective new spouses.

We meet them again in Paris some time later and it is immediately clear that the old pattern is reasserting itself. They are in the middle of a gigantic free-for-all when Victor and Sybil arrive. Later the two couples make up and agree to act in a civilised fashion. Elyot and Amanda vow to be as sensible and civilised as the other two. However, at breakfast it is the correct couple who are at each other's throats. Whatever Elyot and Amanda suffer from, it seems to be catching! Once again they sneak away, vowing never to part—or even argue.

* * * *

The film version was made by M-G-M in 1931.

CREDITS

Producer	Albert Lewin
Director	Sidney Franklin
Screenplay	Hans Kraly, Richard Schayer
	and Claudine West
Photography	Ray Binger

CAST

Sybil Chase	Una Merkel
Elyot Chase	Robert Montgomery
Victor Prynne	Reginald Denny
Amanda Prynne	Norma Shearer
Oscar	Jean Hersholt
Page	George Davis

The film took forty days to shoot, cost $500,000 and earned a $256,000 profit.

* * * *

The Vortex may have seized public attention by the scruff of the neck, but it was *Private Lives* which first had the critics reaching to Sheridan and Congreve for their comparisons. It was brittle and bitchy, urbane and articulate—all the qualities which rapidly became synonymous with "a Noël Coward play."

Even before its New York engagement, M-G-M's head of production, Irving Thalberg, snapped up the property as a vehicle for his wife, Norma Shearer. He also saw it as a way to demonstrate that the fledgling sound film form could not only speak but had something to say. For the first time at least *some* of Noël's dialogue would be heard in a film.

There were those who saw the play as nothing more than a collection of lines. Thalberg's London representative sent him the script with a covering note that read, "If this will make a film, I'll eat it."

Two stories emerge from the transition from script to screen, though neither can be verified. One is that Thalberg arranged for a performance of the New York original to be filmed as a guide for his chosen performers—something that certainly happened with *Cavalcade*. The other is that Noël and Gertie actually auditioned for the parts, but the Thalberg "family" connection made the outcome inevitable. Whether either or both of these events actually occurred, no evidence remains. As late as 1970 Adrianne Allen "seemed to remember" the cameras arriving at the theatre. Noël's response—at a televised seminar honouring him at the National Film Theatre—was that "Adrianne *always* remembered cameras arriving," a remark which effectively deflected the discussion. It may have been Noël choosing to misremember; in any case, it was the *American* production, not the English, that was supposedly filmed.

The balance of evidence suggests that there *was* a filmed version (now lost) made in 1931, which (Norma Shearer's biographer, Gavin Lambert asserts) Thalberg screened for director Sidney Franklin "to provide a blueprint of the pacing and diagramming of scenes, the timing of individual lines for laughter and dramatic impact." It was apparently Thalberg's practice at the time to film a performance of every Broadway property the studio bought—hence, filming *Private Lives* was the rule rather than the exception.

The sadness is that the one opportunity to see Noël and Gertie on film has now been lost. Both would go on to make separate film appearances but there would be no joint ventures. There was a story (almost certainly apocryphal) that Noël was once approached by Hollywood to write a screenplay based on the life of Sarah Bernhardt in which Gertie would star. He is supposed to have replied with one of his cryptic telegrams:

REGRET UNABLE TO WRITE LIFE OF BERNHARDT FOR GERTRUDE LAWRENCE. TOO BUSY WRITING LIFE OF ST. THERESA FOR MAE WEST.

In the July 1931 issue of *Vanity Fair* it was reported that Alfred Lunt and Lynn Fontanne had agreed to appear in the film after making *The Guardsman*. Instead, they elected to return to the stage. (The Lunts found Hollywood no more to their taste than Noël. As Lynn remarked when they left for home: "We can be bought but we won't be bored.")

Surprisingly, most of the play's original structure was left intact, except that the Paris location of the second act was exchanged for a Swiss ski chalet. However, once again, one is left wondering why it took *three* writers to adapt the work of one.

The pairing of Shearer with Robert Montgomery was the fourth of five in as many years and, while their performance is not to be compared with the originals, some of the feistiness of Elyot and Amanda seemed to get through to this rather more laid back couple. During the celebrated "sofa fight" in Act Two Shearer was sufficiently into the role of Amanda to land a punch that knocked Montgomery through a screen. Although she was distraught at her own unladylike behaviour, the take so amused Franklin that he kept it in the final cut.

"What are you doing here?" "I'm on my honeymoon." "That's funny—so am I." Elyot (Robert Montgomery) and Amanda (Norma Shearer) re-create the roles made famous by Noël and Gertrude Lawrence.

The previously-wed newlyweds run off with each other and end up in a Swiss chalet, where their distinctly aggressive approach to affection breaks out once more—this time to be witnessed by their current spouses, Victor (Reginald Denny) and Sybil (Una Merkel).

In *Past Conditional* (1965) Noël describes the prevalent custom of the private viewing:

> In those days in Hollywood no private party was complete without a full length epic beginning before you had gulped down your coffee. It was all done with the greatest style and comfort. The guests settled themselves in vast arm-chairs with drinks on small tables at their elbows. A screen either rose noiselessly from the floor or came down from the ceiling or swung into view on hinged bookshelves and there you were luxuriously stuck for a minimum of two hours. If you happened to have seen that particular movie before it was just too bad, but in fairness it must be admitted that this contingency seldom arose. The film exhibited was invariably brand new and usually starred your hostess which was all very well if you enjoyed it but embarrassing if you didn't. Happily for me the majority of my hostesses were good actesses and most of the movies excellent but there is no denying that those sybaritic evenings were conversationally arid. In addition to these nocturnal distractions there was the daily dose of celluloid to be digested. I never set foot in a studio without being led almost immediately to a projection room where I was installed in the usual vast arm-chair with a drink at my elbow and shown whole films, half films, rough-cuts and rushes.

* * * *

Montgomery was understandably nervous to be playing Noël, in effect. Noël recalled his first viewing of the film in a Hollywood projection room. "I remember that just as the lights went out Bob, who was sitting next to me, slipped into my hand an expensive watch with my initials on it. "This," he hissed, "is to prevent you from saying what you *really* think of my performance!" It didn't, because I thought his and Norma's performance charming and was not

required to dissemble. At all events it was a beguiling and typical gesture."

Looking at the film today, it's easy to see that the "test" version may have proved a mixed blessing. Franklin can be seen to be taking too many pains to film the famous Balcony Scene "classically." To give the lines their due weight—and perhaps to allow for laughter—he creates long pauses and holds close-ups far longer than is necessary. Having got the set piece out of the way, though, he appears to relax and let everyone enjoy themselves. Act 2 is far more freewheeling and we are no longer aware of "editorial intrusion." The director clearly feels he is back in the business of making movies and not filming alien stage dramas.

Grateful to see that the film had respected the original, the critics were uniformly kind. *Motion Picture* magazine recorded that "Norma Shearer matches Robert Montgomery's well-known flair for light comedy and, after the posey dramatics of late, reveals herself as a charming comedienne." Reviewer Mordaunt Hall in the *New York Times* found Shearer's "an alert, sharp portrayal. She appears to have been inspired by the scintillating dialogue . . . it is her outstanding performance in talking pictures . . . and one of the most intelligent comedies to have come to the screen." *Photoplay* magazine: "Well, they've kept them all in—those swell lines of the Noël Coward play. And they're both there—those two grand, impossible, delightful characters . . . A wild farce idea made snappy by a sparkling and at times questionable dialogue." *Time* magazine: "In this production . . . Shearer and Montgomery play through the almost actor-proof situations of the comedy with *savoir faire* which equals, if it does not excel, that of their predecessors."

Several reviewers noted that Shearer sometimes imitated Gertrude Lawrence's mannerisms so closely that she left little room to express her own distinctive personality. Lambert finds her "strained and fidgety." The roles clearly affected both actors, since the *Times* was to note, when the film opened at the Empire, Leicester Square, in February 1932, that "Mr. Robert Montgomery seems rather taken aback to discover that his lines, usually so amiable, have, in this instance, taken on a catty and quite ungentlemanly venom."

There was one aspect of the film process that turned out to be a lot less attractive than it first seemed. Flushed with the immediate success of the play and Thalberg's offer, Coward sold the rights to M-G-M for what seemed at the time a great deal of money. The deal was outright and in perpetuity and it was the same kind many authors made in those days. What neither he nor his agent (Jack Wilson) noticed was the small print that read: "and any other rights of mechanical reproduction." In 1931 TV was no more than a gleam in a technician's eye and videotape a concept waiting to be invented. The result, however, was that, to this day, any other film or electronic version of *Private Lives* or *Bitter Sweet* await the pleasure of the present owners of M-G-M.

*　*　*　*

A French version of the play was filmed in 1936, directed by Marc Allégret.

Sybil Chase (Lucie)	Marie Glory
Elyot Chase (Daniel)	André Luguet
Victor Prynne (Victor)	Heusi Guisol
Amanda Prynne (Annette)	Gaby Morlay

TONIGHT IS OURS (1932)

The film was a remake of *The Queen Was in the Parlour*. It was made by Paramount and first shown in London at the Plaza cinema in March 1933.

CREDITS
Director	Stuart Walker
Associate Director	Mitchell Leisen
Screenplay	Edwin Justus Mayer
Photography	Karl Struss

CAST
Nadya	Claudette Colbert
Sabien	Fredric March
Grand Duchess Emilie	Alison Skipworth
Prince Keri	Paul Cavanagh
General Krish	Arthur Byron
Zana	Ethel Griffies
Seminoff	Clay Clement
Alex	Warburton Gamble
Delegate	Edwin Maxwell

* * * *

"On her wedding night she gave her love to another man" ran the headline on one of the ads, which didn't auger particularly well for the second sound adaptation of a Coward play. As it turned out, the team of Claudette Colbert and Fredric March—used to playing together in several successful earlier films—gave the film a perfectly competent sub-Lubitsch gloss without ever convincing that they were anything but Hollywood stars.

The story sticks close to the original until the *dénouement*, when a group of unusually amiable revolutionaries stroll into the palace to point out that all they really want are a few more rights. If the queen wants to marry a commoner instead of Prince Keri, that's fine with them. Revolution over. This conveniently prevents Sabien, who emerges from Nadya's bed chamber, from facing the firing squad and allows Prince Keri to go off with his own real inamorata. Only General Krish seems to be left feeling that something is rotten in the state of Krayia—but then, this *is* Ruritania.

Richard Watts Jr. of the *New York Herald Tribune* criticised Stuart Walker's heavy-handed direction and bemoaned the absence of the "thistledown" quality an Ernst Lubitsch or a René Clair might have brought to it. In general, Colbert received more compliments for her wardrobe and the loving attention paid to lighting her than she did for her acting. The *New York Daily News* noted: "Some of Miss Colbert's close-ups are ravishing and more than a few damsels in the audience sighed over Fredric March's handsome profile during the hottest of the love scenes," but the *New York World Telegram and Sun* was more pragmatic: "At no time . . . is there any evidence of the intelligence, showmanship, and wit that

*Noël's "one and only expedition into Ruritania"—Hollywood style. The high-born Nadya
(Claudette Colbert) has met and fallen in love with commoner Sabien (Fredric March),
knowing that it is her destiny to marry royalty to save her throne.*

have established Mr. Coward as one of the most brilliant playwrights of the day."

The film did not fare well at the box office and Paramount did not pair March and Colbert together again.

Noël was no more happy with this version than he had been with its silent predecessor:

> The second was made in Hollywood, and was called *One Wonderful Night* or *One Glorious Night* or *One Night of Something or Other.* I saw it once by accident in Washington and left the cinema exhausted from the strain of trying to disentangle my own dialogue from the utter mediocrity that the Paramount screen writers had added to it. It was performed doggedly by Claudette Colbert and Frederic March who were so obviously bogged down by the script that I felt nothing but an embarrassed sympathy for them.

CAVALCADE (1932)

The play was written in 1930 and 1931 and produced at the Theatre Royal, Drury Lane, in October 1931, where it ran for 405 performances.

PLAY SYNOPSIS

The basic structure of the play depicts the parallel upstairs/downstairs lives of the Marryots and their servants, the Bridges, between 1899 and 1929. It opens with Robert and Jane Marryot celebrating the New Year in their London house. The Boer War occupies everyone's thoughts and Robert may soon have to go. For the moment they try to put this to one side, as they celebrate with their two sons and Bridges and his wife, Ellen. It is, after all, the start of a new century.

A month later we are at the docks, as the two women take leave of their respective menfolk. A band on the quayside plays "Soldiers of the Queen."

The war continues. Back at the Marryots the two boys (Edward and Joe) are playing soldiers. Jane's nerves are clearly on edge and her friend, Margaret, insists that she take an evening off and join her at the theatre. Reluctantly, Jane agrees. Margaret goes off to dress, while in the street outside a barrel-organ plays "Soldiers of the Queen."

The two women are watching *Mirabelle*—a pastiche of many of the shows of the period—involving royal birth and mistaken identity. In the middle of the finale, the theatre manager stops the show to announce that Mafeking has been relieved. Pandemonium and relief sweep the audience.

Below stairs at the Marryots the staff are preparing a party to celebrate Bridges's return. When he arrives with Ellen, he announces that he has invested his savings in a pub so that he and Ellen can be independent. The celebration is qualified by the arrival of a newspaper carrying the news that Queen Victoria is dying.

Not long after, both families are watching the funeral *cortège* pass from their balcony. Robert, who has won the V.C., is part of the procession, much to his sons' delight. Everyone stands to attention as the coffin passes and Joe remarks: "She must have been a very *little* lady." Soon after Robert is knighted.

It is some years later. Jane has brought Edward (now 18) to see Ellen in the Bridges' pub. Fanny, their daughter, is dancing to entertain the guests but Bridges himself is inexplicably absent. When he does arrive, he is clearly drunk. There is a scene and Jane and Edward leave. Bridges angrily turns on his family.

Some hours later and Fanny is dancing to a street band outside the pub. Bridges comes out to grab her and in the scuffle he is run over and killed.

A few years later at a popular seaside resort, Jane, Margaret and Joe run into Ellen and Fanny, who has won a concert party talent competition. Ellen tells them that she has kept the pub and that Fanny wants to go on the stage. As they stand chatting, one of those new-fangled aeroplanes flies overhead.

It is now 1912. Edward has married Margaret's daughter, Edith, and they are taking a cruise for their honeymoon. Leaning over the rail, they talk about the life they will share. As they leave, she picks up her cloak to reveal the name *S.S. Titanic* on the life belt. The orchestra softly plays "Nearer, My God, to Thee."

August 1914. War is imminent and Robert and Joe are anxious to enlist. Jane cannot share their excitement. As Robert proposes a toast, she replies: "Drink . . . to victory and defeat, and stupid, tragic sorrow . . . but leave me out of it."

A chronicle of British life from the turn of the century to the then (1930) present day, Cavalcade *was also the inspiration for* Upstairs, Downstairs. *The plot followed the lives of the Marryots—Jane (Diana Wynyard) and Robert (Clive Brook)—and their servants, the Bridges—Alfred (Herbert Mundin, left) and Ellen (Una O'Connor, right).*

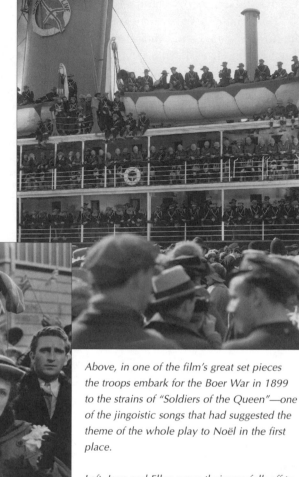

Above, in one of the film's great set pieces the troops embark for the Boer War in 1899 to the strains of "Soldiers of the Queen"—one of the jingoistic songs that had suggested the theme of the whole play to Noël in the first place.

Left, Jane and Ellen wave their menfolk off to war.

October 1918 and Joe is dining with Fanny, now a successful young actress. He wants to get engaged before he has to return to the Front but she, knowing the family opposition they will face, suggests they wait until the war is over.

Later that evening Jane is seeing Joe off at the railway station. The soldiers are singing, their womenfolk crying. It is all too reminiscent of the Boer War for her. She lights a cigarette and turns her back on it.

November 11, 1918. Jane receives a visit from Ellen, who has found out about the affair between Joe and Fanny. Jane replies that they had better wait until Joe returns to discuss the matter further. Ellen takes this as an indication that Jane doesn't believe Fanny is a suitable wife for her son and a row ensues that is interrupted by the arrival of a telegram. They needn't worry about Fanny and Joe any more, Jane tells Ellen—because Joe won't be coming home.

New Year's Eve 1929. The Marryots, now elderly but distinguished, welcome the New Year as they always do, with a toast proposed by Jane to the future of England—"The hope that one day this country of ours, which we love so much, will find dignity and greatness, and peace again."

In the final scene the whole cast are in a night club on an evening in 1930. At the piano Fanny sings "Twentieth Century Blues," a bitter song which suggests that the fulfillment of Jane's wishes may not be easy to accomplish.

* * * *

The film version was made in Hollywood by the Fox Film Company in 1932.

CREDITS

Director	Frank Lloyd
	(who replaced Frank Borzage early in the filming)
Screenplay	Reginald Berkeley

CAST

Jane Marryot	Diana Wynyard
Robert Marryot	Clive Brook
Alfred Bridges	Herbert Mundin
Ellen Bridges	Una O'Connor
Joey Marryot	Frank Lawton
Edward Marryot	John Warburton
Fanny Bridges	Ursula Jeans
Margaret Harris	Irene Browne
Edith Harris	Margaret Lindsay
Annie Grainger	Merle Tottenham
George Grainger	Billy Bevan
The Cook	Beryl Mercer
Mrs. Snapper	Tempe Piggot

THE CHILDREN

Edward Marryot	Dick Henderson, Jr.
Joey Marryot	Douglas Scott
Edith Harris	Sheila MacGill
Fanny Bridges	Bonita Granville

The film was shown at the Tivoli in London in February 1933. *Variety* called it "a dignified and beautiful spectacle . . . a big, brave and beautiful picture," while the *New York Daily News* found it "a magnificent achievement . . . with drama, pathos, tenderness and thrill." "It is unfurled," gushed the *New York Times*, "with such marked good taste and restraint that many an eye will be misty after witnessing this production." Louella Parsons considered it "greater even than *Birth of a Nation*." It won three Oscars in that year—for Best Picture, Best Director and Best Art Direction. Just as important—it took in $3.5 million at the box office.

* * * *

In some ways Noël was perhaps prouder of *Cavalcade* than anything else he wrote. Years later at one of the endless buffet suppers he attended, another guest wondered aloud why only Noël appeared to have been given a fork.

"Well," replied Noël—as if the explanation was blindingly obvious—"I *did* write *Cavalcade*, you know."

He was naturally concerned that, when the inevitable happened and the play was adapted for the screen, it should escape what he believed to have been the fate of his earlier work. In 1941 he could write: "Of all my plays only one, *Cavalcade*, had been filmed with taste and integrity. The rest, with the possible exception of *Private Lives*, which was passable, had been re-written by incompetent hacks, vulgarised by incompetent directors and reduced to common fatuity."

After the unseemly rush to film three of his plays in one year (1927), he was a little surprised when *Cavalcade* was not filmed right away. In fact—"The sale of the *Cavalcade* movie rights had occurred long after the play opened, actually only a few weeks before it closed. I thought, in common with every-one else connected with the production, that of all the plays I had ever written, *Cavalcade* was the most likely to be snapped up immediately, since it could, with the minimum of effort, have been adapted for the screen practically as it was. The cinema Moguls, however, thought otherwise. *Cavalcade* was relentlessly turned down by all the major studios in Hollywood and London."

In the event, a small coincidence triggered the sale. During the last weeks of the play's run a Mrs. Tinker, an American lady, happened to be in London and accompanied a friend to Drury Lane. Noël picks up the story:

> She was so impressed by the play that, on returning to her hotel she immediate-ly sent a cable to Mr. Tinker, urging him to acquire the film rights at all costs. Mr. Tinker had recently been elected as one of the Directors of the Fox Studios and, obviously aware that he had married a remarkably intelligent woman, put her suggestion before the Board. Not having been present I cannot vouch for the accuracy of what I have been told took place. Apparently, Mr. Tinker was swift-ly snubbed for his pains and the suggestion arbitrarily dismissed. However, dear Mr. Tinker, whom sad to say I never met, was obviously not the type of man who cares to have his opinions summarily ignored; in addition to which he was very rich, and it was thanks to his financial intervention that Fox Studios had evaded bankruptcy by the skin of their perfectly capped teeth. I like to imagine that there was a strong dramatic Galsworthian scene in course of which Mr. Tinker, purple in the face, delivered a blistering tirade, hammered on the desk with his clenched fist and finally by sheer force of Right over Might won his point and sank down in his chair mopping his face with a bandana handkerchief, but I fear that the reality was more prosaic.
>
> At all events he did win his point and bitterly against its will, Fox Films capitulated. A week or so later, evidently having decided that they might as well be hung for a sheep as for a lamb, they sent over to London a posse of camera-men and cameras and assistant directors and production managers and, possibly, clapper boys to film the play as it was presented on stage. (Actually a very sensi-ble procedure and I could only wish that other Hollywood studios would adopt it.) This resulted in three days intensive work and my beloved company earning a lot of extra money. Having gone this far Fox considered that it had done enough. Tinkers or no Tinkers and beyond engaging an English director called

Armistice Night and the crowds celebrate in Trafalgar Square.

Frank Lloyd, who I believe had been wandering unemployed through the Hollywood limbo for some time, they washed their hands of the whole affair and turned their dangerous attention to more important matters.

This, of course, was the greatest luck of all. Had they been enthusiastic about *Cavalcade* it would inevitably have been ruined. Millions would have been spent; scads of script-writers would have been engaged to change the play beyond all recognition; stars of grotesque unsuitability would have been asked to play the leading parts; Ace directors would have been hired and fired left and right and the result would have been an epic Hollywood shambles. As it was, their sulky withdrawal from the situation enabled Frank Lloyd, who was a brilliant director, to carry on with his job without indeed much encouragement but also without interference. He proceeded to engage an excellent cast headed by Diana Wynyard, Clive Brook, Frank Lawton, Ursula Jeans, Una O'Connor and Irene Browne (the latter two actresses having played in the London production), none of whom could be described as top-flight Hollywood stars and all of whom were first rate actors. The picture was shot within a reasonable time and I believe stayed more or less within its financial budget. It was also shot in almost cloistered seclusion. Few, if any, top executives' wives and sweethearts and friends were invited onto the set to stand about and gape and get in everyone's way, although it would delight me to think that Mr. and Mrs. Tinker had been granted full access at all times and been provided with canvas chairs with their names emblazoned on them in gold.

It was only I believe when the picture was in its last days of shooting that word got around that it was liable to be fairly sensational and all the little Foxes scurried out of their embossed leather holes and began to sniff around and clamber onto the bandwagon. When at last it had been titled and dubbed and shown secretly in Fox's projection rooms, the jig was up. Rumour has it that a very bright young man who had ardently supported the film at one of the initial conferences and been immediately fired was hurriedly re-engaged with an astronomical rise in salary. I devoutly hope that this is true but fear it is apochryphal.

Noël himself felt the final film was "superior in every way than if I personally had been connected with the actual production." He had one reservation: "I am not favourable to the horsemen going through the wood interpolated as an expression of the passage of time. It is too much like the pages of a calendar being torn off and I feel it hinders the action a little." On the other hand, he did approve of one scene that was not in the play: "The producers of the film decided to allow Joey Marryot to meet his father in Flanders and this I found effective and charming." Most charming of all, though, he found Diana Wynyard as Jane Marryot. He considered her performance "as sincere and beautiful . . . as I had hoped to see in the picturisation of my play. I think I shall always see her standing in Trafalgar Square or saying goodbye to the last of her sons at the station. Yes, Jane-Diana-Marryot-Wynyard will always live for me, as I am sure she will for all those who go to see *Cavalcade*."

*   *   *   *

There was to be one more film version (of sorts). On October 5, 1955 CBS-TV produced a television film on the *Twentieth Century-Fox Hour* which, minus the commercials, attempted to tell the story of the island race in just forty-four minutes.

CREDITS

Producer	Otto Lang
Director	Lewis Allen
Screenplay	Peter Packer
Introduced by	Joseph Cotten

CAST

Robert Marryot	Michael Wilding
Jane Marryot	Merle Oberon
Edith Harris	Marcia Henderson
Fanny Bridges	Caroline Jones
Bridges	Noel Drayton
Ellen	Nora O'Mahoney
Mrs. Snapper	Doris Lloyd
Margaret Harris	Victoria Warde
Joey Marryot	Richard Lupino
Edward Marryot	John Irving

The film was generally released in British cinemas in 1956. It also went under the title *Heart of a Woman*.

DESIGN FOR LIVING (1933)

The play was written in 1932 and originally produced in 1933 at the Ethel Barrymore Theatre, New York, where it ran for 135 performances. The original stars were Noël Coward, Alfred Lunt and Lynn Fontanne.

PLAY SYNOPSIS

Gilda, an interior decorator, lives with Otto, a painter, in his Paris studio. Although they love each other, they believe marriage would spoil their relationship. Gilda receives a visit from Ernest, a picture dealer, who tells her their mutual friend, Leo, has just arrived from America. What, he wonders, will Otto think about that? Will he be jealous of his old friend's success?

Otto arrives from a painting trip. He senses something is wrong but allows himself to be sent off to meet Leo at his hotel. No sooner has he left than Leo appears from the bedroom. He and Gilda discuss the situation. They love each other but they both love Otto too much to hurt him. Leo admits he has always been jealous of Gilda's preferring Otto. Otto returns unexpectedly and everything is admitted. Leo arrived early and . . . Otto makes himself furious and storms out.

Gilda and Leo are now living in London, where Leo is a successful playwright. Leo suggests they get married but she refuses—"Otto would hate it." She still feels their three lives are somehow inextricably linked. But, Leo concludes, there is something missing—and refuses to elaborate.

Later Gilda is alone when Otto arrives and now she knows what Leo meant. The missing piece was Otto. In his desperation at losing her he had taken a long sea voyage to sort out his thoughts. Gilda realises that Otto has matured; he is no longer the weaker of the two men. Should she renew her affair with him? He convinces her that the ordinary rules don't apply to the three of them—"A gay, ironic chance threw the three of us together and tied our lives into a tight knot at the outset. The only thing left is to enjoy it thoroughly." Which they proceed to do.

Ernest calls to see Gilda and tell her that he is moving permanently to New York. Gilda seems in a strange mood. Perhaps she'll join him there. She tells him that she is also going away—to live a life of her own. She leaves letters for Leo and Otto. No sooner has she gone that Otto emerges from the bedroom, just as Leo had done in Paris. At which point, Leo returns. Reading their identical notes—"Goodbye, my clever little dear . . . Thank you for the keys of the city"—they realise they have *both* lost her. They proceed to get drunk and finally burst into tears on each other's shoulders.

New York two years later and Gilda has now married Ernest. She is hosting a cocktail party in her high rise apartment when Leo and Otto are announced and proceed to shock the conventional guests by their unconventional conversation. As everyone is leaving, Gilda slips them a key and tells them to return later. After they leave, she has a sudden realisation of what she seems about to be restarting and leaves hastily by the fire escape.

Next morning Ernest arrives back from a business trip. He is somewhat surprised to see Otto and Leo enter wearing his pajamas. Where is Gilda?

They explain that she has disappeared. Why are they here? They have come for Gilda—she belongs to them just as they belong to her. Gilda then returns, having made up her mind that she must accept the inevitable. The three of them try to explain to Ernest, who works himself up into a rage—as all Gilda's men appear to do—and storms out. The trio look at each other in apparent surprise at this bizarre behaviour, then sit down and roar with laughter. They are still laughing as the curtain falls, though just what they are laughing at is not clear. Ernest? Life's rich pageant? Themselves?

* * * *

The film version was made by Paramount in 1933.

CREDITS
Producer/Director	Ernst Lubitsch
Screenplay	Ben Hecht
Photography	Victor Milner
Art Direction	Hans Dreier

CAST
Tom Chambers	Fredric March
George Curtis	Gary Cooper
Gilda Farrell	Miriam Hopkins
Max Plunkett	Edward Everett Horton
Mr. Douglas	Franklin Pangborn
Lisping Secretary	Isabel Jewel
Mr. Egelbauer	Harry Dunkinson
Mrs. Egelbauer	Helena Phillips
Fat Man	James Donlin
First Manager	Vernon Steele
Second Manager	Thomas Braidon
Housekeeper	Jane Darwell
Mr. Burton	Armand Kaliz
Proprietress of Café	Adrienne d'Ambricourt
Max's Butler	Wyndham Standing
Conductor	Emile Chautard
Tom's Secretary	Nora Cecil
Boy	George Savidan

* * * *

Once again the material proved intractable when the time came to translate it to the screen. Perhaps because it was written to be played by three particular actors who knew each other instinctively and played it as one, but mostly because by now Coward's plays had their being in a parallel universe every bit as artificial as Restoration comedy or the more recent wit of Wilde. Let in a little logic and you bring them crashing to earth. The plays were never about plot, yet time and again that's all the films were left with.

Gilda (Miriam Hopkins), George (Gary Cooper, left) and Tom (Fredric March, right) are the screen versions of Gilda, Otto and Leo in Ernst Lubitsch's 1933 film. Above, the new ménage-à-trois, suitably tidied up for 1930s film audiences and the Hays Office Code. Those were not the only changes. Scriptwriter Ben Hecht claimed to have removed all but one line of Noël's original dialogue.

Design for Living was another subject that had the increasingly powerful film censor to contend with. The virtual *ménage-à-trois* of the original would clearly never pass scrutiny, so a complete makeover was necessary. Leo and Otto became Tom Chambers (Fredric March), a promising playwright—perhaps a tip of the hat to Noël—and George Curtis (Gary Cooper), a budding painter. (Douglas Fairbanks, Jr. was originally cast as George but was taken ill before shooting began.) Gilda (Miriam Hopkins) at least kept the name she was born with but was now gainfully employed as a commercial artist. Screenplay writer, Ben Hecht, made the rather bizarre claim that in the finished script he had removed all but one line of Noël's dialogue—and frankly, it showed. As for the play's core relationship, deference to the Legion of Decency reduced it to a sort of gentlemen's agreement between rival swains, completely ruling out sex.

The critics were positively underwhelmed. The *New York Times* was the most charitable: "Notwithstanding the fact that Mr. Coward's clever lines were tossed to the four winds and that the whole action of the story is materially changed, Mr. Lubitsch, who knows his motion picture as few others do, has in this offering, fashioned a most entertaining and highly sophisticated subject, wherein his own sly humour is constantly in evidence." Richard Watts, Jr. in the *New York Herald Tribune* lamented that Miss Hopkins—at the time a major Paramount investment property—failed to bring to the part "the air of sparkling grandeur which Miss Fontanne introduced."

Weary of it all? Gary Cooper and Fredric March seem to have read the film's reviews.

Hopkins' own memory of the film was not exactly memorable. She recalled the scene on the train "where I wore a hat that clung to the head and came down over one eye. I remember telling myself—'Oh, goodie, now I'll look like Dietrich.'" If she did, no one seemed to notice. The film was a watershed for its two male stars, too. March, deciding that to stay at Paramount was to see himself typecast in more films that would bear banners such as "March adds crowning glory to his brilliant string of romantic smashes," left the studio to freelance. Cooper, realising that conventional romantic parts were not his forte, turned to the homespun roles that lasted the rest of a long career. At least the film, with its elegant emptiness, redesigned the professional living of its two main stars.

In retrospect, there was one other piece of poor casting—director Ernst Lubitsch. Deft as he was in handling subjects that reflected his Middle European background of sly, whimsical introspection, he never fully understood the English Puritan tradition against which Coward's characters were rebelling and on which he was commenting. By reducing it to a classic comedy of manners he was missing the essential dimension of the play.

BITTER SWEET (1933 AND 1940)

The play was written in 1928–29 and originally called *Sari Linden*. It was produced at His Majesty's Theatre, London, where it ran for 697 performances.

PLAY SYNOPSIS

The Marchioness of Shayne is giving a dance at her London house. When the guests break off for dinner, a young engaged couple are left alone, except for the pianist, Vincent. The girl (Dolly) doesn't seem to be particularly convinced of their future happiness. They discuss their spirited elderly hostess, whom Dolly really admires and a row ensues, which ends with her fiancé leaving.

Seeing Dolly alone, Vincent declares his hopeless love for her. As he takes her in his arms, Lady Shayne enters. When the situation is explained to her, she asks Dolly what she intends to do and is exasperated when Dolly doesn't know. As the rest of the guests return, she lectures them on their superficiality. It was not always so. As she speaks, the lights dim and her voice grows younger.

We now find the young Lady Shayne—Sarah Millick—in 1875 as a girl of sixteen, rehearsing for her music teacher, Carl Linden. As the scene progresses, it is clear that he is in love with her. He tells her that he cannot play at her forthcoming wedding; he must go away. Her fiancé, Hugh, enters with her mother, putting an end to the singing lesson. Carl says his goodbyes and leaves. Sarah falls weeping into her mother's arms, much to her fiancé's puzzlement.

Mrs. Millick is giving a ball at which Carl is conducting the orchestra. Everyone notices that Sarah is behaving strangely, almost hysterically—much to Hugh's irritation. When the rest of the guests have gone, Sarah and her girl friends begin to play childish games. In Blind Man's Buff, with Sarah as "it," she bumps into the departing Carl. Unable to restrain himself, he kisses her. When she realises what has happened, she admits her own love for him. With the connivance of the other girls, the two lovers steal away into the night.

"I'll See You Again." Anna Neagle and Fernand Gravey.

Carl (Fernand Gravey) and Sarah —now Sari (Anna Neagle) have eloped to Vienna, where they earn a precarious living playing in a local restaurant. They dream of the day when they'll have a "dear little café" all their own.

We are now in Schlick's café in Vienna five years later. Carl is in charge of the café orchestra and Sari (as she is now called) is a dance hostess. They receive a visit from Captain Lutte, who complains to the proprietor, Herr Schlick, that Sari is offhand with him. If Schlick values his custom and that of his men, he will order the girl to dine privately with him that evening. Hearing of this, Sari begs Carl to leave the café. Something bad is about to happen, she knows. He persuades her that they must stay just a little longer. Soon they will have the money to open their own little café.

That evening the café is crowded. Lutte and his men are drinking heavily. Inevitably, the Captain asks Sari to dance and she refuses. Lutte complains to Schlick, who reminds Sari that she is engaged as a dancing partner. She must dance with whoever asks her or be fired. Later, when Lutte claims his dance, he becomes increasingly amorous. Carl, who has been watching all this from the stage, leaps down and strikes the Captain. There is a duel in which Carl is mortally wounded. He dies in Sari's arms.

Fifteen years have passed. The elderly Lord Shayne is giving a party in London. The guests include Sarah's young girl friends, now respected society matrons. All of them are agog to meet the famous European singer, Sari Linden, Lord Shayne's special guest. Sari enters and is immediately recognised as Sarah, whom they all supposed to be dead. As the evening ends, Lord Shayne proposes to her—not, it seems, for the first time. This time she promises to think it over.

As Sari/Sarah entertains the guests with the song that she and Carl shared ("I'll See You Again"), the lights fade once more.

We are now back in the first scene with Sari (Lady Shayne) as an old woman. Convinced by what she has heard, Dolly goes off with Vincent, just as the young Sarah did. Left alone with her memories, Sari sings:

> *Though my world has gone awry,*
> *Though the end is drawing nigh,*
> *I shall love you till I die,*
> *Goodbye!*

*   *   *   *

The first film version was made in England by British and Dominion Films in 1933 and shown at the Carlton, Haymarket, in September of that year.

The second was made by M-G-M in Hollywood in 1940 in Technicolor.

CREDITS
1933 VERSION

Producer/Director	Herbert Wilcox
Screenplay	Herbert Wilcox, Moncton Hoffe and Lydia Hayward

CAST

Sarah Millick	Anna Neagle
Carl Linden	Fernand Gravey
Capt. August Lutte	Miles Mander
The Footman	Gibb McLaughlin
Herr Schlick	Clifford Heatherley
Hugh Devon	Esmé Percy
Lieutenant Tranisch	Stuart Robertson
Vincent	Hugh Williams
Dolly	Pat Paterson
Henry	Patrick Ludlow
Gussi	Kay Hammond
Mrs. Millick	Norma Walley
Manon Le Crevette	Ivy St. Helier

1940 VERSION

Producer	Victor Saville
Director	W. S. Van Dyke II
Screenplay	Lesser Samuels

CAST

Sarah Millick	Jeanette MacDonald
Carl Linden	Nelson Eddy
Baron von Tranisch	George Sanders
Lord Shayne	Ian Hunter
Max	Felix Bressart
Harry Daventry	Edward Ashley
Dolly	Lynn Carver
Jane	Diana Lewis
Ernst	Curt Bois
Mrs. Millick	Fay Holden
Herr Schlick	Sig Rumann
Lady Daventry	Janet Beecher
Herr Wyler	Charles Judels
Manon	Veda Ann Borg
Market-Keeper	Herman Bing
Mama Luden	Greta Meyer

* * * *

Noël may have made only one dramatic foray into Ruritania but he made several into the world of operetta (or *operette*, as he preferred to call it). *Bitter Sweet* (1929) was his big early success and he was trying to repeat it as late as *Pacific 1860* (1946) and arguably even *After the Ball* (1954).

Two films were made of it—a British version in 1933 in which director Herbert Wilcox cast his wife, Anna Neagle, in the first of numerous starring vehicles; and an M-G-M travesty of 1940, the fourth of an apparently endless series starring the singing duo Jeanette MacDonald and Nelson Eddy. In neither case did Noël feel his material had been well served but at least the Anna Neagle version was reasonably faithful to the original and proved popular with the domestic audience. It left out the play's third act entirely and moved directly back from 1880 Vienna to the then present day.

The *New York Times* considered it "an artistic production and its scenes are set forth with gratifying elegance and sober fluency to the frequent accompaniment of tuneful music and singing."

The M-G-M version was an altogether different story. Noël records in 1941: "The epic film version . . . in violent Technicolor arrived at the Empire . . . I had already seen it in a projection room in Hollywood and had decided, sensibly, to wipe it from my mind. It was directed with gusto by Mr. Victor Saville [in fact, it was directed by M-G-M contract director, W. S. ("Woody") Van Dyke. Saville was only guilty of producing it] and sung with even more gusto by Miss Jeanette MacDonald and Mr. Nelson Eddy. It was vulgar, lacking in taste and bore little relation to my original story."

He later told a reporter—"I can never revive *Bitter Sweet*. A pity. I was saving it up as an investment for my old age."

The latter point was duly elaborated in the synopsis that the studio issued to accompany the film:

> On the eve of her marriage to Harry Daventry, a pompous young Englishman, Victorian belle Sarah Millick scandalises her family and friends by her unnaturally excited conduct at a ball in London, and then elopes to Vienna with her singing teacher, Carl Linden. There they live in poverty—but happily—among Carl's friends, including Max and Ernst, penniless musicians, who pawn Carl's furniture when all else fails. After an unlucky experience in which they attempt to give music lessons to the child of a market-keeper in exchange for food, Sarah and Carl become street-singers with Max and Ernst at Baden. Carl's hope of selling an operetta he had written to Herr Wyler, the impresario, had met with no response, but fortunes change when Sarah wins the attention of young Lord Shayne and his gambling opponent, Baron von Tranisch, of the Imperial Cavalry. Shayne believes that Sarah's singing brings him luck. Von Tranisch has a more personal romantic interest. He instructs Herr Schlick to hire Sarah as an entertainer in his Vienna café, where Carl is to lead the orchestra. When von Tranisch pays unwelcome attentions to Sarah, she resists. But Daventry, appointed to the Viennese Embassy by now, and Jane, the fluttery but calculating belle who had finally married him, are witnesses to von Tranisch's advances, and report the matter to Carl. He takes no interest in their smug gossip but Sarah refuses to return to the café. There comes a night, however, when Herr

Wyler is believed to be a guest at the café and is willing to hear Carl's operetta. Max and Ernst go to bring Sarah, that she may sing it. But again von Tranisch makes himself offensive. Carl finds himself forced into a duel which he has no hope of winning and von Tranisch runs him though. He dies in the agonised Sarah's arms. She finds new hope, however, in the fact that her friend and benefactor, Lord Shayne, has persuaded Wyler to produce the operetta with her as star. Thus Carl's music will live on through her singing, and every time she sings his music she will feel that he is with her.

Not only was the story line altered but, to accommodate stars who were happier singing than acting, several of the key songs were reallocated. For instance, Eddy appropriates "Tokay," and some non-Coward material is even added.

Noël saw it for the first time in the autumn of that year just before leaving for Australia. From the ship he wrote to his secretary, Lorn Loraine:

> I spent one night in Hollywood but I utilized it by sitting in a projecting room and seeing the film . . . No human tongue could ever describe what Mr. Victor Saville, Miss Jeanette MacDonald and Mr. Nelson Eddy have done to it between them. It is, on all counts, far and away the worst picture I have ever seen. MacDonald and Eddy sing relentlessly from beginning to end looking like a rawhide suitcase and a rocking horse respectively. Sari never gets old or even middle aged. "Zigeuner" is a rip snorting production number with millions of Hungarian dancers. There is no Manon at all. Miss M. elects to sing "Ladies of the Town" and both Manon's songs. She also dances a Can-Can!
> . . . At one point in Old Vienna she offers Carl a cocktail! . . . It is the vulgarest, dullest vilest muck up that I have ever seen in my life. It is in Technicolor and Miss M.'s hair gets redder and redder until you want to scream. Oh dear, money or no money, I wish we'd hung on to that veto.

WE WERE DANCING (1942)

"We Were Dancing" was one of the nine one act plays in *Tonight at 8:30.* Described as "A Comedy in Two Scenes," it was first produced at the Phoenix Theatre, London, on January 29, 1936.

PLOT SYNOPSIS

The scene is the Country Club at Samolo, Coward's mythical South Sea island under the British flag. A dance is under way. On to the terrace come a couple, Louise Charteris and Karl Sandys, dancing together. They kiss and don't even notice when Louise's husband, Hubert, and his sister, Clare, come and find them. When she tries to introduce the two men, she finds she does not even know her partner's name. Hubert asks her to leave with him and she refuses. She and Karl—as she now knows him to be—are violently in love, she says.

Karl explains more about his background. He is in the family shipping business and the following Wednesday he sails. Louise declares that she will go with him, even though the prospect seems less glamorous than it did to begin with. Hubert demands to know how they can be so sure of their feelings for each other. She replies in song:

> *We were dancing,*
> *And the music and lights were enhancing*
> *Our desire.*
> *When the world caught on fire,*
> *We were dancing . . .*

Overcome with emotion, she faints in Karl's arms. They try to revive her, just as the orchestra starts to play the National Anthem. She manages to stand to attention with the others.

The four of them talk all night. Louise tries to persuade Karl to go to South Africa instead of Australia but he refuses. Eventually, Hubert and his sister leave, Hubert asking Karl to make Louise happy. Alone now, the two look at each other and see that they are, in reality, perfect strangers. Even when they dance together in the cold light of morning, the magic has gone. Sadly, they go their separate ways.

*   *   *   *

The film version was produced by M-G-M in 1942. It was described in the credits as being "based in part" on the play by Noël Coward.

CREDITS

Producer	Robert Z. Leonard and Orville Dull
Director	Robert Z. Leonard
Screenplay	Claudine West, Hans Rameau and George Froeschel
Photography	Robert Planck
Music	Bronislau Kaper

CAST

Vicki Wilomirska	Norma Shearer
Nicki Prax	Melvyn Douglas
Linda Wayne	Gail Patrick
Hubert Tyler	Lee Bowman
Judge Sidney Hawkes	Marjorie Main
Mayor Tyler-Blane	Reginald Owen
Grand Duke Basil	Alan Mowbray
Mrs. Vanderlip	Florence Bates
Mrs. Tyler-Blane	Heather Thatcher
Olive Ransome	Connie Gilchrist
Mrs. Bentley	Nella Walker
Mrs. Charteris	Florence Shirley
Mr. Bryce-Carew	Russell Hicks
Mrs. Bryce-Carew	Norma Varden

Ava Gardner made her feature film debut in a bit part.

The synopsis issued to critics reviewing the film shows how little resemblance it bore to the original play.

SYNOPSIS

When she falls in love at first sight with impecunious but irresistible Nicki Prax (an Austrian baron), Vicki Wilomirska (a Polish princess) breaks off her engagement to wealthy Hubert Tyler, even though she knows that Nicki, like herself, is a professional house-guest and they will have to live on their charm. Accordingly, they conceal their marriage and meet in secret until Linda Wayne, a fashionable decorator and one of Nicki's old flames, reveals their secret. They are finally reduced to being guests of the newly-rich. Nicki determines to look for a job and put their marriage on a respectable basis.

A particularly attractive invitation, however, proves his undoing, for, when they decide to make this one last house-party stay, Vicki finds Linda pursuing her husband. She brokenheartedly sues for a divorce, and although Nicki defends himself ably and passionately, Hubert, acting as Vicki's lawyer, wins her the divorce. Again Vicki becomes engaged to Hubert and they plan the decorating of a home Hubert has built for his intended bride.

But Nicki appears on the scene again. With the now-repentant Linda's help, he has arranged to get a job with the firm decorating the new house. At first behaving impersonally, he finally breaks down and confesses that he loves no one but Vicki. Vicki says it is too late. At the Palm Beach betrothal party Nicki comes to say farewell. The musicians strike up a tune. It is a waltz to which they danced when they first eloped; they waltz again, they kiss once more—and they elope!

* * * *

The critics agreed that it was a "romantic comedy produced in high style" with the *New York Times* adding with a touch of irony that "According to the credits, it is based on a couple of one-act plays by Noël Coward. And indeed it does have a brittle quality characteristic of his work."

This was the last film M-G-M was to make of a Noël Coward property. If the result wasn't as dire as *Bitter Sweet*, nor was it as competent as *Private Lives*, despite the huge strides in production quality that had been achieved in the past decade.

The clue lies in the telling phrase "based in part." The initial premise of two people falling instantly in love when they dance and the occasional underlining reprise of the Coward music are just about the only vestiges of the original play. Elsewhere there is a hint of "Ways and Means"—another of the *Tonight at 8:30* plays—as Vicki and Nicki turn into professional and impoverished house guests. The hostess who finally calls their bluff is called Olive, the same name as the character in that particular piece. That apart, the characters of the two leads owe a great deal to Elyot and Amanda in their edgy bickering and their can't-live-*with*-can't live-*without*-each-other quality.

After *Private Lives* Norma Shearer clearly fancied herself as a Coward heroine—so much so that she gave up the part of Mrs. Miniver that won Greer Garson the Oscar that year to do so. But by this time her creative guardian angel, husband Irving Thalberg, was dead and the quality of the studio's output was suffering accordingly, especially when it came to literate drama. The world was at war and the appetite for soufflés was missing,

Robert Z. Leonard's We Were Dancing *(1942): Impecunious professional charmer Nicki Prax (Melvyn Douglas) causes Polish princess Vicki Wilomirska (Norma Shearer) to break off her "suitable" engagement to marry him. For plot reasons, they keep their marriage secret.*

especially soufflés that resolutely refused to rise. It was effectively the end of Shearer's career but as she herself admitted later: "Nobody but myself was trying to do me in."

"You should hear Miss Shearer snap a frigid 'Quiet!'" said critic Bosley Crowther, who considered she "acts with dazzling aplomb and wears clothes that will knock your eyes out." Melvyn Douglas, he felt, "turns in another of his devilishly debonair jobs . . . But the story sags too often and is dragged out in tiresome length." *Time* concluded the piece was "tailor-made for Miss Shearer, who has been off the screen for a year." Having said that, it concluded that "*Dancing* is a costly, embarrassing picture, whose mood and manners are both dated and false." But it was *Photoplay*—normally a staunch Shearer supporter—that administered the *coup de grâce:* "Too utterly utter and all that sort of rot, my deah!"

Shearer's biographer, Gavin Lambert, reflected in 1990 that "Today her performance looks strenuously artificial, and all its energy seems directed to preserving an illusion of youth." Miss Shearer, it will be remembered, played Juliet at the age of thirty-six in the 1936 George Cukor *Romeo and Juliet* opposite the forty-three-year old Romeo of Leslie Howard.

Noël described the piece as "a light episode, little more than a curtain-raiser. It was never intended to be anything more than this and, unlike its author, it fulfilled its promise admirably." Miss Shearer—standing in for Gertie for the second time—on this occasion did not. "She's a gay, laughing Shearer again," the ads proclaimed. On this occasion there was too little to laugh at.

* * * *

There was to be one interesting footnote to the "pre-war" period that passed largely unnoticed. On July 28, 1939, NBC-TV put on a live television production of *Hay Fever*. With a running time of eighty minutes it was the first play to be adapted at full length for the fledgling medium.

CREDITS
Producer/Director   Edward Sobol

CAST
Judith Bliss   Isobel Elson
David Bliss   Dennis Hoey
Simon Bliss   Montgomery Clift
Sorel Bliss   Virginia Campbell

* * * *

There is something of a first shall be last—or at least, latest—irony about *Hay Fever*.

Over the years there have been sporadic attempts to turn it into a film. In 1965 Celia Johnson—who had just ended her run in the National Theatre revival, where she took over from Edith Evans—wrote teasingly to Noël, "Now you know that I can play comedy a bit." She went on to wonder, apparently ingenuously, "Have they ever made a film of it? I suppose they must have. Just a thought." And it was a very good thought, which should have been snapped up.

As it was, it had to wait for the 1990s, when a series of attempts were made to put a suitable "package" together, all of them fated to be frustrated at the last moment by lack of financing.

For many years the driving force behind it was producer Roger Peters, who had the ambition to put on record the performance of Maggie Smith as Judith Bliss. Smith had never played the part, although she had understudied Dame Edith Evans in the famous 1964 revival at the National Theatre that had marked the beginning of the renaissance of Noël's theatrical reputation. There had been more than one occasion during the run when the dame's temperament—not to mention her command of the lines—had almost handed the stage over to her stand-in and no one who had seen the rehearsals for that eventuality was in any doubt that, young as she was, "the Smith gal" was a Judith Bliss-in-waiting.

When the latest project began a quarter of a century later, Dame Maggie (as she then was) declared herself distinctly interested but the endless delays proved to be too much. In the late 1990s she decided she was "too old for the part." Even though it was pointed out that she was not as old as Evans had been, the argument proved unpersuasive and even counter-productive. Evans had had the advantage of discreet stage lighting and makeup—not the remorseless eye of the film camera lens.

Exit Dame Maggie . . . but the quest continued. At length the way through the financial woods, at least, was pointed by director John Boorman. For years Boorman had been making his idiosyncratic films from the tax advantageous base of Ireland and offered his services in helping the production do the same.

In late 1999 it was announced that Judith would now be Joanna Lumley—fresh from her TV success in *Absolutely Fabulous* and an experienced Coward actress—with Jonathan Lynn directing, production to commence in the spring of 2000. By then Peters had departed and the money had turned into Irish fairy gold. After a several year gestation period, the project was put to rest—at least for now.

* * * *

Centenary Year (1999) brought rumours of several movie intentions. Tom Cruise and his then wife, Nicole Kidman, were to make *Blithe Spirit* for Universal—with, of course, some "adjustments." Options were taken out—or at least explored—on *Quadrille, Easy Virtue, Present Laughter, The Vortex, The Young Idea* and *I'll Leave It to You.* In the event the only one that came to anything turned out to be *Relative Values.*

RELATIVE VALUES (2000)

The film was given its premiere at the Odeon, Leicester Square, on June 21, 2000.

CREDITS
Produced by Overseas Film Group/Midsummer Films

Producer	Christopher Milburn
Director	Eric Styles
Screenplay	Paul Rattigan and Michael Walker
Music	John Debney

CAST

Felicity, Countess of Marshwood	Julie Andrews
Nigel, Earl of Marshwood	Edward Atterton
Don Lucas	William Baldwin
Peter	Colin Firth
Crestwell	Stephen Fry
Moxie	Sophie Thompson
Miranda Frayle	Jeanne Tripplehorn
Elizabeth	Stephanie Beacham

STORY

The Countess of Marshwood is awaiting the arrival of her son and heir, Nigel, and his fiancée, the Hollywood film star Miranda Frayle. When they are married she intends to give the running of the estate over to them, though she has her doubts about the marriage. The one person who seems excessively upset by the prospect is Moxie, the Countess's longtime maid. We soon find out why. Miranda Frayle is Moxie's younger sister, who has remade herself in Hollywood, having been "no better than she should be." To save Moxie's social embarrassment, it is decided that she should pose as a wealthy friend of the Countess.

When Miranda arrives, she doesn't recognize her older sister and proceeds to tell a fanciful account of her own tragic upbringing. Matters are further complicated by the arrival of Don Lucas, her co-star and former lover, who is determined to stop her from marrying Nigel. The machinations of the various members of the Marshwood household, both upstairs and down, soon create the circumstances that persuade Miranda to give up Nigel and return with Don to the one place where you can be who you want to be.

* * * *

You suspect you're in trouble when the credits herald "A Christopher Milburn Production" and "An Eric Styles Film"; you know with increasing certainty when, in addition to the two main producers, the film is produced in association with "Starz Encore Entertainment, The Isle of Man Film

Commission, Lucinda Films, The Film Republic and Silvercreek"—the very kind of cooperative enterprise that had caused Noël so much pain in the beginning of his film career.

To add insult to injury, the film doesn't even use Coward music. The opening sequence is cut to Rodgers and Hammerstein's "It's Almost Like Being in Love" and the subsequent "incidental" music is just that.

Julie Andrews is clearly uncomfortable and lacks the steely hand in the velvet social glove that the part of the countess demands, while the rest of the cast behave as though they were being directed in a 1950s British "B" picture. As Crestwell, the butler/philosopher, says at one point, "Comedies of manners swiftly become obsolete when there are no longer any manners." They also become obsolete when there is no comedy.

Variety's Derek Elley summed up general critical opinion when he concluded, "Individual performances and Coward's neatly turned dialogue just about make the pic go the distance, triumphing over unimaginative direction and an awkward screenplay."

PART TWO

A Noël Coward Production

As you will be interested but not surprised to hear, I loathe the whole Film business as much as I ever did, if not more. But never again am I going to sell my plays to the movies without having the whole thing controlled by my own unit.

—*A letter from Noël to the Lunts*

ALL MY PLAYS EXCEPTING CAVALCADE HAVE BEEN VULGARIZED DISTORTED AND RUINED BY MOVIE MINDS AM NOW MIDDLE-AGED AND PRESTIGE AND QUALITY OF MY WORK ARE MY ONLY ASSETS FOR THE FUTURE THEREFORE HAVE DECIDED HENCEFORWARD NEVER TO SELL FILM RIGHTS UNLESS I HAVE ABSOLUTE CONTROL OF SCRIPT DIALOGUE CAST TREATMENT DIRECTOR CAMERAMAN CUTTER AND PUBLICITY CONVINCED PRESENT UNAVOIDABLE LOSS IN FUTURE INEVITABLE GAIN.

—*Cable to business manager Jack Wilson*

*"Good luck, sir . . ." The few survivors of the Tryon—played by real sailors—
say their goodbyes to Capt. "D" in Alexandria.*

A few days after the *Blithe Spirit* opening (1941), a deputation of three gentlemen, Filippo del Giudice, Anthony Havelock-Allan and Charles Thorpe, called on me at the Savoy Hotel. I received them warily because I knew that the object of their visit was to persuade me to make a film, and I had no intention of making a film then or at any other time. I had generated in my mind a strong prejudice against the moving-picture business, a prejudice compounded of small personal experience and considerable intellectual snobbery. I had convinced myself, with easy sophistry, that it was a soul-destroying industry in which actors of mediocre talent were publicised and idolised beyond their deserts, and authors, talented or otherwise, were automatically massacred.

—Future Indefinite

IN WHICH WE SERVE (1942)

An original film script written in 1941 and produced by Two Cities at Denham Studios. First shown in London at the Gaumont, Haymarket, and the Marble Arch Pavilion simultaneously on September 27, 1942.

CREDITS

Producer	Noël Coward
Associate Producer	Anthony Havelock-Allan
Directors	Noël Coward and David Lean
Assistant Director	Michael Anderson
Screenplay	Noël Coward
Photography	Ronald Neame
Art Director	David Rawnsley
Art Supervisor	Gladys Calthrop
Music	Noël Coward
Editors	David Lean and Thelma Myers

CAST

Capt. "D" Kinross	Noël Coward
Shorty Blake	John Mills
Walter Hardy	Bernard Miles
Alix (Mrs. Kinross)	Celia Johnson
Mrs. Hardy	Joyce Carey
Freda Lewis	Kay Walsh
"Number One"	Derek Elphinstone

"Flags"	Michael Wilding
"Guns"	Robert Sanson
"Torps"	Philip Friend
Doctor	James Donald
Engineer Commander	Ballard Berkeley
"Snotty"	Chimno Branson
Sub-Lieutenant R.N.V.R.	Kenneth Carten
Mr. Blake	George Carney
Mrs. Blake	Kathleen Harrison
Uncle Fred	Wally Patch
Young Stoker	Richard Attenborough
Maureen Fenwick	Penelope Dudley Ward
Pilot	Hubert Gregg
Edgecombe	Frederick Piper
Brodie	Caven Watson
Coxswain	Johnnie Schofield
A.B. Joey Mackridge	Geoffrey Hibbert
A.B. Hollett	John Boxer
Parkinson	Leslie Dwyer
Colonel Lumsden	Walter Fitzgerald
Captain Jasper Fry	Gerald Case
Mrs. Lemon	Dora Gregory
Reynolds	Lionel Grose
Mr. Scatterthwaite	Norman Pierce
Lavinia	Ann Stephens
Bobby	Daniel Massey
May Blake	Jill Stephens
Mrs. Farrell	Eileen Peel
Mrs. Macadoo	Barbara Waring
Barmaid	Kay Young
Freda's Baby	Juliet Mills

* * * *

In July 1941 Noël received a visit from Filippo del Giudice and Anthony Havelock-Allan, the principals of Two Cities Films. He was perfectly well aware of what these two gentlemen had in mind: "The actual proposition they put to me was that if I agreed to write and appear in a picture for them I should have complete control of cast, director, subject, cameraman, etc., and that all financial aspects would be, they assured me, settled to my satisfaction once I had consented. It would have been churlish not to appreciate that this was a very flattering offer indeed, and although all my instincts were against it, I was forced to admit to myself that, provided I could think of a suitable idea, there was a good deal to be said for it."

The two men were accompanied by Charles Thorpe of Columbia Pictures, who had £60,000 of his company's money ready to back the producer's offer.

He did not have to wait long for the idea to arrive. The following evening he dined with his old friend, Louis Mountbatten, then a senior figure in the Admiralty.

After dinner, he told me the whole story of the sinking of the *Kelly* off the island of Crete. He told it without apparent emotion, but the emotion was there, poignantly behind every word he uttered. I was profoundly moved and impressed. The Royal Navy . . . means a great deal to me, and here, in this Odyssey of one destroyer, was the very essence of it. All the true sentiment, the comedy, the tragedy, the casual valiance, the unvaunted heroism, the sadness without tears and the pride without end. Later on that night, in my bed at the Savoy, I knew that this was a story to tell if only I could tell it without sentimentality but with simplicity and truth.

Within the next few weeks *In Which We Serve* was conceived, although it was not until much later, after passing through various metamorphoses, that it achieved its final script form. (*One working title was White Ensign.*) The first stumbling-block was that although Dickie was all for a film which would be good propaganda for the Navy, he was not unnaturally afraid of my basing my story too exactly on the *Kelly*, lest the film should in any sense become a boost for himself. After I had reassured him on this point, and in particular had made it clear that I had no intention of copying his own particular character, he undertook that he and some of the survivors of the *Kelly* would give me that help without which it would have been very difficult to have produced a convincing film. First of all, the Royal Navy's permission was asked for and willingly given. Dickie's personal enthusiasm cut through many strings of red tape and set many wheels turning on my behalf. From the beginning he saw the idea as a tribute to the Service he loved, and he supported me through every difficulty and crisis until the picture was completed. But that happy moment was over a year away and, in the meantime, there were many tiresome obstacles to be surmounted. I could never have surmounted them without his constructive criticism, his gift for concentration, his confidence in the film and in me. This might so easily have been strained beyond bearing within the ensuing few months, for neither of us dreamed in those first days of enthusiasm what a variety of dim-witted ogres we should have to vanquish. To begin with, the Press, led exultantly by the section which had proved hostile to me before, proceeded to sabotage the project from the moment the news broke that I was going to do it. There were sneering articles, contemptuous little innuendoes in the gossip columns, letters of protest written, I suspect, editorially, and the suggestion that I was going to portray Lord Louis Mountbatten on the screen, a suggestion for which no possible evidence had been furnished, was reiterated *ad nauseam* until even the Admiralty became restive and, I believe, although I am not certain, protested strongly to the Ministry of Information. I only know that after a few weeks the clamour died down. The fact that there had never been any question of my portraying Lord Louis Mountbatten on the screen was, of course, ignored. "Captain (D)" in *In Which We Serve* was conceived, written and acted to the best of my ability as an average naval officer, whereas Mountbatten was then and is now, very far from being an average naval officer. He is definitely one of the most outstanding men

British Lion PRESENTS NOEL

"IN WHICH W

Directed by NOEL COWARD & DAVID LEAN

Photographed by RONALD NEAME

NOEL COWARD

BERNARD MILES .

JOYCE CAREY

COWARD'S

"...VE SERVE"

A TWO CITIES FILM

...OHN MILLS

...LIA JOHNSON

...AY WALSH

His heart has sneaked up on Mr. Coward . . . here is a subtle warmth in the old astringency. For the first time he seems to be speaking, not to the select but to the simple.
—C. A. Lejeune
The Observer

of our times and showed every sign of becoming so when I first knew him in the early 'twenties. My "Captain (D)" was a simpler character altogether, far less gifted than he, far less complicated, but in no way, I hope, less gallant. The story of the film was certainly based on *H.M.S. Kelly*, for the simple reason that through Mountbatten himself, and his shipmates who survived, I was able to get first-hand information and accurate details, both technical and psychological. The story, however, could have applied to any other destroyer sunk in action during the war. In all of them were the same potentialities, the same bravery, the same humour and the same spirit.

In a letter to Mountbatten in September he reports that he has informed the Admiralty that "I shall be doing tests of myself as Captain 'D' for a month before we start the actual shooting. These will be shown to anyone in the Admiralty who wishes to see them and if they then feel that I am unsuitable for the part there will be time to get somebody else." He goes on to assure him that "I have got the best camera man and the best cutter in the business and everything is under control." (David Lean might have bridled at the "cutter" description even then.) "I hope all this bloody publicity won't annoy you as much as it annoys me. My voices tell me that disapproval of the project comes from very high up indeed. It is flattering to have such powerful enemies."

In his *Autobiography* Noël continues:

It would be wearisome to recapitulate all the irritations, frustrations and tiresomeness which had to be coped with during those difficult weeks. It would also involve undignified recrimination and possibly several libel suits. One thing I cannot forbear to mention was a letter to the Lords of the Admiralty from the head of the film department in the Ministry of Information. This letter, written on receipt of the final script, stated unequivocally that in the Ministry's opinion the story was exceedingly bad propaganda for the Navy, as it showed one of H.M.'s ships being sunk by enemy action, and that permission would never be granted for it to be shown outside this country. The contents of this letter were communicated to me over the telephone by the head of the Ministry of Information's film department (Jack Beddington) and, I need hardly say, left me speechless with rage. It was also made known by some means or other to the Two Cities Film Company, which had already invested a great deal of money in the production. The information, naturally enough, terrified them, and if I had not acted quickly the whole project would probably have been abandoned, at considerable financial loss, a few weeks before the actual shooting was due to begin. Fortunately for me this serious setback occurred later in the production of the picture, when Mountbatten was back in England again, having been recalled from his command of the *Illustrious* to take over Combined Operations. I telephoned him immediately and he asked me to have a script delivered to him right away, and that he would show it to the Member of the Board of Admiralty who would be most likely to be called upon to make a decision in this matter. This gallant Admiral, who was afterwards lost in action, took the view that the story was very good propaganda indeed and that the fact that the film portrayed a destroyer being sunk in war-time was certainly not necessarily a reflection on the Navy, where so many gallant ships were fighting to the end in the defence of the country's vital sea-lines of communication.

So, upheld by this moral support, Dickie and I went to the Ministry of Information, where we were received by Brendan Bracken, who kindly sent for the writer of the letter. Dickie went off like a time bomb and it was one of the most startling and satisfactory scenes I have ever witnessed. I actually felt a pang of compassion for the wretched official, who wilted under the tirade like a tallow candle before a strong fire. The upshot of it all was that from that moment onwards I had to endure no more nonsense from the Ministry of Information. In the following September, when *In Which We Serve* opened at the Gaumont, I received a congratulatory letter from this very official saying that the film was as moving and impressive as he had always known it would be. A curious missive.

In the meantime the Two Cities Film Company's fluttering hearts were stilled and on we went with the production [which lasted from February 5th to June 27th, 1942].

On looking back on the seven months between the original conception of *In Which We Serve* and the day on which we actually began shooting, I find I can see them only in terms of montage—endless conferences; hours in Wardour Street projection-rooms looking at British films; casting discussions, technical discussions; days at sea in destroyers; drives to and from Denham Studios in winter weather; arguments about the budget of the picture; moving into a dank cottage so as to be

near the studios; crises, triumphs, despairs, exaltations; tests in the Gaumont British studios at Shepherds Bush; hours of staring at myself on the screen—heavy jowls, no eyes at all; lighting wrong, lighting better; visits to shipyards in Newcastle; to dockyards at Plymouth and Portsmouth; endless discussions with experts—naval experts, film experts, shipbuilding experts, gunnery experts . . .

On February 5th, 1942, we had our first shooting day of *In Which We Serve*. David and Ronnie and I were quivering with nerves, but, as the day went on, they evaporated as they usually do under stress of intensive work, and in the evening we had a drink in my dressing-room to celebrate the fact that at last, at long last, our preliminary troubles were over and we were under way.

* * * *

Mountbatten's personal role in the making of the film was decisive. On one hand he cleared the decks, so to speak, so that the film could be made at all. He made sure that the king read the screen play at an early stage, and there was great relief when it was learned that His Majesty found Noël's approach a positive and appealing way of dealing with the subject. Yes, a British ship was lost, but at the same time the essential spirit of the Royal Navy was exemplified by the character and behaviour of the men depicted, and the convoy of ships shown in the final sequence symbolised both the power and resolution of the Senior Service when the need arose.

Mountbatten himself was concerned throughout that the film—although originally inspired by the fate of the *Kelly*—should be seen as a parable of the service as a whole.

In September 1941 he urged Noël to make a statement that the *Tryon* was "equally based on the *Cossack* and destroyers that took part in Dunkirk (which the *Kelly* did not) . . . whereas I am naturally proud that the story is in part based on the *Kelly*, I am sufficiently jealous of my own reputation in the Navy to wish to avoid personal publicity in this connection."

Noël did what he could to bring that about. The first draft script had Kinross married to Lady Celia, living in a large country house with a Rolls-Royce and a chauffeur. Noël was persuaded to rethink and eventually came to describe them as "Ordinary upper middle class family. Private income, £600 or £700 a year. Small country house outside Plymouth, ordinary, pleasant wife, family, one boy and one girl, Cocker spaniel called Trafalgar." The Rolls was exchanged for a Ford and the chauffeur fired.

As the film progressed, Mountbatten seemed to forget his personal concerns and put the needs of the film first. He took a leading part in the casting of the actors and those who knew both men claimed that in many of Kinross's speeches Noël was quoting his friend almost verbatim. He even wore Mountbatten's naval cap when playing the part.

The eventual and universally positive reaction to the film clearly pleased and relieved Mountbatten greatly but before the public gave their verdict, there was one important "preview." The film owed much to the agreement of the Second Sea Lord—the Admiralty's Head of Naval Personnel—to lend a ship's company. With the film under way, Mountbatten recalled:

Noël very tactfully asked him to come and visit the shooting. He came down, was very impressed by the men and afterwards Noël said would he like to see some of the rushes. He agreed, and they showed him the scene . . . when the Ordinary Seaman, played by John Mills, had to go and tell the Chief Petty Officer, played by Bernard Miles, that he had a letter from his young wife to say that Bernard Miles' wife had been killed in an air-raid in Plymouth. A very moving scene. The Admiral was very emotional. "By jove, Coward," he said, "that convinces me you were right to ask for a proper ship's company, *real* sailors. No actors could possibly have done that.

The politics of obtaining permission to make the film at all were a temporary distraction from the other consideration that was concerning Noël—his own lack of film experience. He was the first to admit that he knew nothing about the technical side of directing a film. With his usual professionalism, he set out to study the subject.

Nearly thirty years later he recalled those days for a National Film Theatre audience: "I wasn't particularly impressed with British pictures at the time, so I took myself to a viewing room and twice a day for two weeks I saw every British film that was available." When he came to look at the notes he'd made, "I found that just about every credit for cutting a film was David Lean, most of the photography was someone called Ronald Neame and the

Will the real Capt. "D" stand up, please? Noël compares notes with his friend Lord Louis Mountbatten, on whom the character was based. Mountbatten was ambivalent about the identification—until he saw the film!

general production was Anthony Havelock-Allan. So I asked David Lean to come and see me. When he came, I told him I'd like him to work on the film. He said he'd do it with pleasure but he insisted on co-directing. People stiffened like a Bateman drawing, until I said—'Oh, please *do!*' It was David who directed the picture. I took the actors aside occasionally."

Not surprisingly, perhaps, recollections of key incidents tend to differ after so long.

On the funding of the film, Bernard Miles—who was chosen by Mountbatten personally—remembered that a 'Jewish carpet merchant' called Sassoon presented del Giudice with a cheque for £195,000 before filming began, leaving the production free and clear. Ronald Neame recounts a very different and more romantic version in which del Giudice came along ten days into shooting, pleading abject poverty and claiming that the whole venture to date had been done on credit. Would Lean please cut together the first twenty minutes that he had already shot so that it could be shown to Sam Smith, head of British Lion film distributors? Seeing little alternative, Lean did so and—according to Neame—that clinched the British Lion decision to fund the rest of the film.

The facts seem to be that, as costs escalated, various backers backed out. Columbia withdrew at £100,000, to be replaced by C. M. Woolf of General Film Distributors. When the budget reached an estimated £180,000, GFD withdrew and it was at that point that British Lion stepped in to fund a film that finally cost £200,000.

Although contemporary accounts do not record the fact, the story did not end there. At some point film producer Sir Alexander Korda became involved and persuaded United Artists to join a consortium of backers. In October 1942—when the film was safely and successfully launched—he sent Noël a copy of a cable he had received:

> WHEN YOU FORCED US TO INVEST ONE HUNDRED THOUSAND POUNDS IN A MOTION PICTURE I THOUGHT WE HAD ALL GONE CRAZY BUT YOU PROBABLY MADE ONE OF THE GREATEST CONTRIBUTIONS TO UNITED ARTISTS EVER MADE BECAUSE QUOTE IN WHICH WE SERVE UNQUOTE IS POSITIVELY SENSATIONAL AND HARDBOILED. THOSE WHO HAVE SEEN IT ACCLAIM IT A MRS. MINIVER ON A BATTLESHIP CONGRATULATIONS AND THANKS.

Korda's accompanying comment: "I thought it would amuse you as, in spite of the perfectly idiotic expression, the fact still remains that they still like your picture."

*   *   *   *

There are also different accounts of how Lean came to be chosen. While Noël liked it to be thought that he had unearthed him personally and while it is certainly true that his was the final decision, it seems likely that the decisive opinion was director Carol Reed's. Reed, some two years older than Lean, was also making his reputation in the 1940s and by the end of the decade the two men were vying for the reputation as the best British director with the press keenly encouraging rumours of a personal rivalry that was greatly overstated. Not long after the successful opening of *In Which We Serve*, Reed was having dinner with John Mills. "You know, when Noël Coward went around asking for suggestions as to who should help him with this film, I suggested David Lean." He added ruefully, "It's the most insidious goddam thing I ever did."

Later, when he had seen the finished film, he wrote to Noël: "Never have I been more moved or excited by any Picture—No acting in film has ever been better . . . I have just left Alex Korda who thought it perfect—we both said we hoped you were pleased enough to come back and do more of them—and then we were silent for a while—we got awfully depressed and drank to our own future."

Noël's recollection of how Lean came to be involved was turned over time into a polished anecdote. Lean himself was inclined to remember it variously. In some interviews Noël agreed gracefully after a moment's thought. In others the "I agree" was said "rather snappily." Lean did have another card up his sleeve, an offer to work on the next Powell and Pressburger film—but only as editor. There was no doubt in his mind as to his preference but it did give him the courage to express his conviction.

Director David Lean (left) confers with Nöel in the "tank." Every day he would dive in to set an example. On the last day of shooting he remarked: "There's dysentery in every ripple."

Then there was the evolution of the storyline. Lean and Havelock-Allan were summoned to Noël's Gerald Road studio, where they found Gladys Calthrop and another friend of his, actress Joyce Carey. To this audience Noël read his first attempt at the script on which he had worked with novelist and playwright Clemence Dane. At that point it was called *White Ensign*.

WHITE ENSIGN

ROUGH OUTLINE

This is the story of a ship and it is dedicated to the Royal Navy, "upon whom, under the good providence of God, the wealth, happiness and prosperity of this country does chiefly depend."

The ship is *H.M.S. Tryon*, the leader of the 35th Destroyer Flotilla, the other ships of which are, respectively, *H.M.S. Tempest*, *H.M.S. Typhoon*, *H.M.S. Tornado*, *H.M.S. Thunderbolt*, 69th Division, and *H.M.S. Terrific*, *H.M.S. Trusty*, *H.M.S. Turbulent* and *H.M.S. Tenacious*, 70th Division.

The leading characters in the story are Captain E. V. Kinross, R.N. (Captain "D"), Chief Bosun's Mate, Walter Hardy (Chief Buffer) and Ordinary Seaman J. A. Blake (Shorty). The real hero, however, is the ship, *H.M.S. Tryon*; perhaps one should say "heroine" because ships, no matter how belligerent, are always, unaccountably, female.

The story begins on a quiet day in March 1937 in a Tyneside shipyard when the keel of the *Tryon* is laid. In the course of the following year until 1938, when she is ready for launching, it might be effective to show briefly, in montage, various outstanding events of that year, always referring back to the progressive construction of the ship. In 1938 she is launched by Lady Alexander Kinross who, according to custom, breaks a bottle of champagne across her bow and says—"God bless this ship and all who sail in her." (This exact phrasing to be verified.) From this moment onwards there should be further montage shots—Berchtesgarten, Munich, etc., also the introduction of the leading characters—widely separated and unaware of one another's existence.

First of all, Walter Hardy, who has just been rated Chief Petty Officer and is an instructor at the Royal Naval Barracks, Plymouth. He is a man of about thirty-eight, Plymouth born, and he lives with his wife, Doris, at No. 17 Renown St. Doris, altho' fond of him, is rather whiney and given to much complaint over very little. He has been in the service since the age of fifteen, when he was on the *Impregnable*, a boys' training ship. He has been far afield and passed dutifully through the various stages of promotion. At the moment (1938) he is becoming restless at having a shore job and itching to get to sea again. In May 1939 he goes to Tyneside to "build ship" at Grayson-Kemsley Yard. ("To build ship": Anyone who goes to a ship before completion can say— "When I built the so-and-so" or "I stood by the so-and-so when she was building." The skeleton crew which ultimately takes the ship from Tyneside to her base is known as "Navigating Party.")

Shorty Blake, when we first see him, is a deck hand on one of the Prince Line freight and passenger ships—we might catch him for a moment almost anywhere . . . Indian Ocean . . . Southern Pacific. He is a cheerful young cockney in his early twenties.

Edward Kinross we see for the first time in Hong Kong, where he is commander of a battleship. His promotion to Captain has just come through and in February 1939, the night before he sails for England in a P&O liner, his brother officers give a dinner party in the Wardroom in his honour. This is a gay, rowdy and highly enjoyable occasion showing, at its best, the light side of the service in one of the large ships. Hong Kong harbour at night with ships of all shapes and sizes lying at anchor—ferries bustling to and fro—the Peak stretching up into the sky with the lights of the town below it. The evening finishes with the party clustered round the Wardroom piano (invariably out of tune) singing any shanties they can remember at the top of their lungs. The next morning the P&O liner sails for home.

Edward Kinross is thirty-eight years old when we first see him. He is an average looking, clean cut naval officer. He has had a reasonably distinguished career. In 1925, when he was Flotilla Signals Officer with a destroyer flotilla in the China Station, he met—while on leave in Pekin—Lady Alexander Chatsworth, who was staying with her uncle, the British Minister. In 1926, on his return to England, they were married. She was and is a woman of charm and intelligence and altho' she appears comparatively little in this story, whenever she does, it should be fully realised that she is both in type and behaviour, one of the more admirable representatives of our upper classes. Her affection for her husband is personal and true, sometimes covered by an indulgent mockery. She is gay, witty and quite incapable of shirking any responsibility.

Edward himself (called Teddy by his intimates) is efficient and single tracked in his devotion to his service. He is well liked and respected by the men who serve with him. He makes it his business to consider them and understand them and demands faultless discipline in return. With his brother officers he is popular, altho' they are a little in awe of him. He is seldom bad tempered but can be rather sardonic on occasion.

On his return to England in the spring of 1939 one of the great ambitions of his life is achieved; he is given command of a flotilla, thereinafter becoming Captain "D," 25th Division. We see him journey to the shipyard at Tyneside to join his ship. He takes her through her trials. At the end of her full power trial there is a little ceremony. The shipyard manager comes to the captain and says—"Will you take over the ship?" The captain replies—"Right. I'll sign for her now." He then says—"Chief Bosun's Mate, hoist the white ensign." On the order a dockyard matey in a cloth cap hauls down the red ensign. The Chief Bosun's Mate hoists the white ensign—a whistle is blown— everybody stands facing aft and salutes. The dockyard mateys doff their caps. This whole scene must be done simply and accurately. On the 25th of August the *Tryon* arrives at Plymouth to commission. The commissioning of a destroyer usually takes twenty-one days but on this occasion Kinross, realising that war is imminent, collects the ship's company around him and tells them that in the present urgent circumstances he intends to get the whole job done in three days.

The men respond and work begins at once—nobody sleeps for three nights—the stores are loaded, equipment installed—the whole intricate business of commissioning a ship done at lightning speed. At the end of the allotted time, the *Tryon* sails for Portland or Scapa or any other suitable naval base, where she is painted and the gunnery and torpedoes are installed. A few days after Mr. Chamberlain's declaration of war she sails for the Western approaches—i.e., the stretch between Gibraltar and England. She is at first engaged in U-boat hunting—then in October she is put on escort work.

On December 16 she sights a German freighter, the *Elmshorst*, which is suspected to be carrying over a hundred British merchant marines—the crews of various ships torpedoed in the Atlantic. This incident should be based as nearly as possible on the *Altmark*. Captain "D" pursues and overtakes the ship, draws alongside and has a boarding party leap onto her decks to demand the prisoners.

After a little scuffle the German captain gives in and the men are released, among them Shorty Blake who, in spite of all the privations and horrors and humiliations that have been inflicted on him and his fellow captives, still manages to be reasonably perky. The *Tryon* returns with the released prisoners to Plymouth.

They arrive two days before Christmas. This should be a moving scene and based as closely as possible on the *Altmark's* return. The ship is in port to boiler clean. This means shore leave and we are able to follow the main characters, among them the Chief Bosun (Chief Buffer, Walter Hardy) and Shorty, who has decided, on the voyage home, to join the Navy. Walter Hardy has promised, if possible, to ask for him to be rated to the *Tryon* when his training is completed. The Captain stays on board with half the ship's officers. His wife arrives on Christmas Eve with a Christmas tree for the Wardroom.

Christmas Day should be contrasted in the three different atmospheres—Shorty's with his cockney family in Peabody Buildings, Pimlico . . . Walter's with his wife and wife's family in Renown St., Plymouth . . . and the Captain's on board with his officers and some of their wives. In the forenoon he entertains the Petty Officers and Leading Seamen in the Wardroom—beer and cigarettes. In the evening the Christmas tree party is given, also in the Wardroom.

Soon after Christmas the *Tryon* sails again, this time on the North Sea Patrol, where she encounters extremely bad weather. On one occasion she is plunging about in a heavy sea and does a spectacular roll of 50 degrees. The Torpedo lieutenant is having his breakfast in the Wardroom—actually he is standing, holding on with both hands while the Wardroom orderly feeds him through the hatch. When the roll comes his boots leave marks all along the upper deck and he finishes up hanging head downwards with his feet caught in a curtain rail. The Captain is on the bridge and braces himself, although practically upside down. (These two shots should be very effective if they can be successfully faked.)

In April, when the *Tryon* is temporarily in port, Shorty arrives having finished his training on the *Raleigh*. (Shots of which can have been shown earlier.)

He is now an Ordinary Seaman and highly delighted with himself. At the end of May Captain "D" receives orders to proceed to Dunkirk to evacuate exhausted troops. He calls the ship's company together on the forecastle and makes a speech to them to the effect that the job looks as tho' it might be a bit tricky. He finishes by saying that the most dangerous thing is to be the first ship to arrive and asks them which ship it is to be? They all shout— *"Tryon."* He then says the next most dangerous thing is to be the last to leave and which ship is *that* to be? Again they shout *"Tryon."*

The Dunkirk episode should be mainly devoted to the embarking of a battalion of guards. The *Tryon* is alongside the jetty. The guardsmen stream on board—bloodstained, wounded and utterly exhausted after seventeen days and nights of continual fighting with no sleep and hardly any food. In the course of the short voyage back to Dover they all occupy themselves with polishing their buttons, shining their shoes and generally sprucing themselves up. They disembark at Dover, where their regimental band has come to meet them, and march off the ship in perfect order, as if they were changing the guard at Buckingham Palace. The whole ship's company cheers them.

In July the *Tryon* is in a night battle in the North Sea . . . Just as some enemy ships are turning away under smoke, the *Tryon* is hit by a shell and a few seconds later by a torpedo. The shell hits a gun turret, killing every man in it, among these men is Shorty's best pal. Shorty, who is on the way up to the turret with some ship's cocoa, arrives a split second after if has been hit. He finds everyone dead inside, straddles the body of his pal and goes on firing the gun. (This based on a true incident on *H.M.S. Achilles*—Battle of the River Plate.) The torpedo hit almost completely disables the ship but Captain "D" brings her limping home to Tyneside. On arrival in port he summons the ship's company and talks to them. It has been reported to him, he says, that during the action two men left their stations in the engine room. He goes on to explain that this is one of the most punishable of all naval crimes but that unfortunately he cannot punish the two delinquents, because the fact of their leaving their stations was entirely his fault for not having sufficiently impressed his personality on them to make their letting him down impossible.

Following this scene there is a gay interlude ashore when all the ship's officers ask him to dinner in the local hotel—after which they take the entire front row at the Hippodrome and more or less break up the whole show to the delight of the audience and, oddly enough, even the actors.

There should now be a passage of time sequence in montage from July 1940 to April 1941. The object of this being to show the eternal vigilance of the Navy. There would be shots of the ship in calm seas, rough seas—sunshine—snow—pursuing submarines, convoying merchant ships, fighting off air attacks, etc. The officers and men should be shown sometimes unshaven and exhausted after several days without taking their clothes off—at other times spruce and clean, as tho' the thought of war had never crossed their minds. Somewhere during this sequence there should be a brief shot of Captain "D" accompanied by his wife and young son leaving Buckingham Palace after receiving the D.S.O. (Also Shorty doing the same thing, if possible.)

*On his way home on shore leave Shorty (John Mills) meets Freda Lewis
(Kay Walsh), the girl he is to marry.*

In this very rough outline I have purposely omitted the more human aspects
of the story. These will be adapted later to the circumstances.

On April 20 the *Tryon* sails on convoy duty to the Near East and thence to
Malta, where the Flotilla is based. On or about May 20 Captain "D" receives
orders to make rendezvous with the Mediterranean Battle Fleet off Crete. He
calls his commanding officers together. They plan operations. This takes place
in the Captain's cabin aft. The meeting starts pompously, as all such meetings
inevitably do, and loosens up with cocktails and a few jokes (as most of such
meetings inevitably do!).

Twenty-four hours later rendezvous with the Battle Fleet is made . . . It's not
long before they find themselves in a hazardous situation between enemy ships
and the bombardment of the shore. So the *Tryon* is the last to leave. She has not
gone far when the Luftwaffe appear in wave after wave. At first the high altitude
bombing causes little or no danger, then the dive bombing begins.

Finally, after changing course repeatedly to escape being hit, a bomb gets a
direct hit on her when she is doing thirty knots—she completely turns turtle in
fifty seconds. Not a man leaves his station. The gunners continue firing until the
rush of the water tears them away. The Chief Bosun's Mate is knocked uncon-
scious on a gun turret and is flung out of it into the sea. Shorty is swept over-
board. The Captain goes over with the ship but manages to fight his way up to
the surface. He sees a Carley float and shouts to any struggling men who can
hear him to swim to it. Finally, he collects about forty of them on it, among them
Shorty, who has contrived to drag the Chief Bosun's Mate onto the float with

him. Many of the men are wounded and dying—all are covered with black oil fuel. They are machine gunned every few minutes.

The *Tryon* is still on the surface a little way off, keel upwards. Suddenly one of the men shouts—"She's going!" The Captain, who is in the water by the side of the float, hauls himself up and looks towards his ship. He says—"Three cheers for the ship." The men cheer huskily as the *Tryon* disappears from view.

A few days later, when they have been picked up and landed in Alexandria, the Captain calls the men around him for the last time. He says, in effect— "Generally when I make a speech to you I crack a few jokes but today I don't feel like cracking jokes and I don't feel that you would want me to, either. I am sad at the loss of my ship and of the officers and men. But they are all lying down there together and they're in very good company. I should like to say to all of you who are left that there isn't one of you that I should not feel proud and honoured to serve with again."

The next morning—the day before the Captain is due to fly home—the Torpedo Lieutenant. comes and invites him to dine ashore that night with those who are left of the Wardroom officers. The captain accepts, tho' recoiling inwardly at what can only be a depressing, macabre evening. The dinner takes place. There is a round table and ample spacing between each chair for one of those that are missing. There are eight officers present including the Captain. They are all dressed in borrowed, ill-fitting uniforms. The dinner, contrary to Captain "D's" anticipations is strangely gay. The men who have died are discussed ordinarily without emotion, as tho' they were still there. Only at the very end is there just a moment of emotion. Someone leans across to the Captain and says— "A toast." The captain rises—lifts his glass and says, very simply—"The ship." They all rise, lift their glasses and say—"The ship."

And that is the end of the story.

* * * *

Lean remembered:

It lasted for, I don't know, two-and-a-half hours. It was very rambling, contained a lot of dialogue and, at the end of reading it, he said to me, "Well, what do you think of that, my dear? What sort of film will it make?"

I said–"Well, it's simply wonderful, but the trouble is that what you've read me will run for five hours on the screen."

"Oh, my God," Noël is supposed to have replied, "I never thought of that. I thought you could do anything in the movies. I fear this has as many restrictions around it as the stage."

Then Lean made the suggestion that was to shape the whole film. He advised Noël to go and see *Citizen Kane*, Orson Welles's film that had recently won golden opinions from filmmakers and critics around the world and is still consistently top of any ten best list. Noël went that very day and reported back to Lean that he would be back to him with a rewrite within two weeks.

The revised script borrowed Welles's flashback format, using the Carley raft to bring the survivors together. The device enabled Noël to use "some of the best things that he had written in this very, very long version." Lean then turned it into a detailed shooting script that suited his editorial mind. "I used this method, which I later did with other writers, and put it into what I call a sort of blueprint for a film. As you shoot, you may alter it slightly, but it serves as a blueprint at your back all the time."

*   *   *   *

One of the actors Noël had to take aside occasionally was himself. He was well aware that in acting the part of a naval officer, he would have to play very much against type.

"I had to be awfully careful. I act a great deal with my hands—and naval officers do not! I was clasping my hands behind my back, doing *anything* rather than do a 'Noël Coward' gesture."

He was helped immeasurably by the presence of two hundred and fifty sailors on loan from the Royal Naval Barracks in Portsmouth, "so all the drill was accurate and not a lot of actors putting their lanyards in unorthodox places. All had been in action. They knew what I was talking about."

He remembered the final scene where he says goodbye to the remaining crew members of the sunken *Tryon* as being particularly difficult. Part of it was his own technical inexperience. The assembled crew had to part—rather like the Red Sea—to allow the camera to track through for an enormous close-up of Noël, who then had to emote solely to the camera, a challenge to his stage-taught technique that would instinctively have him embrace the whole audience. The moves he could learn. The hard part was in expressing the emotion itself:

> I found it very, very difficult to adapt myself—and not to use too much emotion. I had to have the emotion inside and do as little with my face as possible. Because, if I'd done it as I did in the first take we did, I looked emotional. And that was the one thing I didn't want to do. A naval officer, you should feel it in his voice and heart but you would not see it in his face.
>
> After that finale—I had to say goodbye, stand still and say goodbye to each one of them. I had written some things in and I tore up my script and said, "Please, chaps, say what you think you would have said in this situation." And this I could hardly take. Each one of them said their own line, like "Good Luck, sir!" or "Chin up, sir"—all these perfectly trite, ordinary phrases, spoken from the heart. Talk about improvisation. It was nothing to do with "acting." They were being. But then, it was only a film and only a take. I doubt if they could have got that amount of emotion in, if they'd been playing it eight times a week.

*   *   *   *

Lean was to admit years later that he didn't think Noël was right for the part. Early in the production the "team" had expressed their reservations to del Giudice, who had "had a word with Noël." Noël totally agreed: "I'm not suitable but I'm going to play it." And play it he did. Nonetheless, Lean's verdict remained: "I am swearing in church but I don't think Noël was a good straight actor. It's awfully hard. Noël isn't really a commander . . . as Mountbatten was. And certainly, not as the family man . . . "

As the cameraman, Neame had his share of problems, one of which was how to light the distinctive Coward face. In his *Diary* entry for January 6, 1942, Noël recorded the ultimate solution:

> Day spent doing scenes over and over again to try and eliminate Noël Coward mannerisms. Saw yesterday's rushes and for the first time was pleased with my performance and my appearance. Ronnie has at last discovered what to do about my face, which is to photograph it from above rather than below.

Some of the principal actors—who were also Noël's personal friends—were inclined to share Lean's reservations. Looking back, Richard Attenborough felt that "there was an element of caricature in his performance . . . a certain self-consciousness about the 'private scenes.'" John Mills remembered sitting next to Noël one day during rushes and feeling embarrassed. "He was very, very nervous and very bad in one scene." Then, as if sensing what Mills was feeling, Noël tapped him on the knee. "'Daddy knows,' he said—and we reshot it the next day."

It wasn't long into the shoot before the mechanics of filmmaking began to bore Noël. Once he saw that David Lean knew what he was doing, he left more and more of the actual directing to him, preferring to stay in his dressing room playing *bézique* with Gladys until he was needed in front of the camera.

His several different responsibilities in the overall production brought out the chameleon in him. Cameraman Ronald Neame once had the temerity to ask him why, when he was part of "management," was he often so difficult to deal with as a performer. "When I am an actor," Noël replied tersely, "the actors are my friends. *You* are the enemy."

One stage habit, though, that he enforced rigorously on the film set was that the actors should come knowing their lines. In one sequence he peremptorily fired a small part actor for violating this, creating a problem in the process. Noël immediately pressed the assistant director into service and sent him off to be suitably costumed and to learn his lines. In true film terms the story should end with a star being born. In fact, the temporary actor was Michael Anderson, whose subsequent career was to be *behind* the camera as the director of films such as *Around the World in Eighty Days* in which one of his stars was—Noël Coward (who knew his lines because he wrote them himself!).

> Work on the picture proceeded slowly but steadily. There were good days and bad days, cheerful days and bad-tempered days. There were nine very uncomfortable days when John Mills, Bernard Miles and I, and twenty others, spent from 8:30 a.m. to 6.30 p.m. clinging to a Carley float in a tank of warm but increasingly filthy water; also we were smeared from head to foot with synthetic fuel oil, only a little of which we were able to scrape off for the lunch break.

He was saved at least one major discomfort. The close-up of him struggling under water after the *Tryon* sinks was an out-take from *The Scoundrel*!

Designer Gladys Calthrop, Noël and co-director David Lean inspect the set up of the next shot at Denham Studios. Inset: Camerman Ronald Neame.

Richard Attenborough—who made his debut in the film—remembers the "bad days":

> We were in that tank for something like two to three weeks. The rest of us would hold our noses and lower ourselves into it but not The Master. He would dive in— a little flat perhaps—but in he would dive. On that last day he came to the surface, covered in oil and filth, and said in that distinctive voice—"There's dysentery in every ripple."

Others remember another Coward saying: "A destroyer is the star of this film," he insisted at the beginning of shooting. "There will not be any blondes in the wardroom. Such things never happen in British destroyers—well, rarely."

John Mills has a rather bawdier recollection. While clinging to the raft, his character (Shorty) is strafed by German planes. To create the necessary effect, Props rigged up a device in which a series of condoms were exploded under water. To this day Mills claims to be "the only actor shot in the arm with a French letter." In fact, the only people in any real danger during the sequence were the pilots of the "German" planes doing the apparent strafing over the real (and empty) sea. Part of the "Enemy Flying Circus" of captured planes, they performed in constant fear of being spotted and shot down by the RAF!

Throughout the whole production no detail was too small to escape Noël's attention. For David Lean his professionalism was graphically underlined the day a harmonica player arrived on the set to work on the film's soundtrack. Before long it became clear that the man's talents left much to be desired. Lean observed Noël gazing with awed fascination: "Look at him—the eager look of the inefficient."

The Master was not to have things all his own way, however. West End audiences may have had their ears attuned to his clipped delivery but the same was not true of all the Denham studio technicians. After the speech in which the captain shares with the crew his vision of the *Tryon*—"a happy ship is an efficient ship"—a sound man was heard to ask if someone would please tell Mr. Coward to watch his enunciation during that "fish and chips speech."

*   *   *   *

In Which We Serve—its title taken from the morning prayer said on all Royal Navy ships—was typical of a genre of propaganda films turned out during World War II. The format was invariably the story of a group of men linked by being part of a regiment or ship or plane. We see them in action and, as the story unfolds, we find out more about their private lives. A year before he chose David Lean—and probably one of the reasons he did so—Noël had seen the earlier war film *One of Our Aircraft Is Missing*, which Lean edited. Comparing the two films today, it's easy to see the editor in the director. Both films share the tradition of the British documentary in the way the battle scenes are shot and assembled in montages that alternate images of action—anti-aircraft guns blazing, explosions, planes diving, hands feeding shells into gun muzzles—with reaction shots of individual unidentified combatants, heroically framed. Conflict is defined in details.

The basic structure of the film rearranges past and present. The surviving sailors of the *Tryon* cling to a life raft from which they can see their doomed ship slowly sinking. We then learn their personal backgrounds and their interrelationships as these men, who may well be drowning, reflect on their lives. The oil-stained faces ripple dissolve to small domestic incidents and to earlier times on the ship. In this way the story is revealed in parallel. The device is used in a general rather than a specific sense and it would be pointless in a film of such genuine emotional power to argue whether this character could have known this or that fact at that time. In its own way the blurring of lines reflects the characters' interdependence.

For the first time in a Coward film the irony implicit in the dialogue is reflected in the imagery. Mrs. Kinross peacefully reads to her children from "The Walrus and the Carpenter," but when she gets to the line about the "billows smooth and bright," Lean cuts to a depth charge going off. Later the Kinross family picnic on a sunny cliff top, when suddenly an aerial dogfight takes place overhead. The juxtaposition of a false domestic peace among the realities of war is frequently repeated. But perhaps the bitterest image is that of a floating newspaper bearing a January 1939 date and the headline: "No War This Year" against the discreet caption: "Crete May 23rd 1941." Since the newspaper was the *Daily Express*, it made its owner, Lord Beaverbrook, a lifelong enemy of both Noël and Mountbatten. As it happened, the idea was Havelock-Allan's. It was not in the original script and was only written into the final draft.

Another visual signature Lean imparts to the film is the series of long tracking shots moving into and emphasising a single character but defining the composition of the group en route. The move through the ranks of men at the ship's dedication service to find Kinross, their leader; the track along the party table to hold on Mrs. Kinross, as she grudgingly and publicly accepts the rivalry of her husband's "other woman"—his ship; and, most memorably, during Kinross's farewell to his few surviving shipmates. For the first time in a Coward film—thanks to Lean—the camera becomes a player.

Noël used to refer to the film in later years as his "*Cavalcade* of the sea" and there are certain resemblances in the upstairs/downstairs characters—a social and class division which naval life underscores. The main resonance, though, is in the spirit of fierce patriotism, expressed—as it was in *Cavalcade*—most particularly in the peroration. In place of the earlier play's "Toast to the Future," we have the captain's farewell speech. The film had opened with the narrator's words—an uncredited Leslie Howard speaking them as a favour to Noël—"This is the story of a ship . . ." Kinross completes the thought:

> Here ends the story of a ship, but there will always be other ships, for we are an island race. Through all our centuries the sea has ruled our destiny. There will always be other ships and men to sail in them. It is these men, in peace or war, to whom we owe so much. Above all victories, beyond all loss, in spite of changing values in a changing world, they give, to us their countrymen, eternal and indomitable pride. God bless our ships and all who sail in them.

Critics—particularly those who are too young to have lived through the war—have been inclined in recent years to criticise the film's emotional atti-

tude as overly simplistic. By today's standards they have a point. We now know enough to realise that, while there are undoubtedly two sides in a conflict, even in a Western things are not really as simple as the Good Guys versus the Bad Guys.

The point, however, is irrelevant to an appreciation of the film in its historical context. This was the way a people at war *felt* about the war. The Dunkirk Spirit that Churchill embodied and Noël expressed was what the British people needed to help them survive and win it.

* * * *

The film had its premiere in September 1942.

> The premiere was given in aid of Naval Charities and the preponderance of naval uniforms and gold lace gave considerable *cachet* to the occasion, and I was moved and proud to see the impact of the picture on that distinguished audience. Towards the end there was a great deal of gratifying nose-blowing and one stern-faced Admiral in the row behind me was unashamedly in tears. For me it was a wonderful experience. I had, of course, seen the film in all its phases, but I had never seen it entirely completed nor heard an audience react to it. I felt that it was a fine piece of work which more than justified all the troubles, heartburnings, disappointments and frustrations we had endured in the making of it. There it was, once and for all, well directed, well photographed and well played and, above all, as far as I was concerned, an accurate and sincere tribute to the Royal Navy.

The critics clearly caught the spirit of the film and were prepared to look objectively at the "new" Noël Coward, even though their editorial colleagues had initially condemned his casting and, indeed, the project as a whole.

Dilys Powell in the *Sunday Times* came out unequivocally with:

> *In Which We Serve . . .* is the best film about the war yet made in this country or in America. . . A correspondent very sensibly complained to me the other day that we could hardly blame Hollywood for caricaturing our working people when we caricature them in our own cinema. Well, here is a film in which character scarcely ever slips into caricature. The tradition of English life has imposed on its ruling classes a veneer of good manners and imperturbability which brilliantly conceal surface as well as temperamental individuality; to look like a character thus becomes eccentric. The working and lower middle classes, however, have no such mask, and the temptation for the screen-writer to exaggerate natural individuality until it turns to farce is clear. The story of a destroyer . . . makes a distinction between the superficial smoothness of officers and their wives and the more obvious individuality of petty officers and ordinary seamen, but without denying the first their character and the second their humanity.

In the *Observer* C. A. Lejeune (for once) agreed: "his heart has sneaked up on Mr. Coward. *In Which We Serve* never gushes, but there is a subtle warmth in the old astringency. For the first time he seems to be speaking, not to the select but to the simple."

Ernest Betts—even though he *was* writing for the antipathetic *Daily Express*—found it "Human, deeply moving . . . brutally faithful and exact," while the *News of the World* claimed: "This is Hollywood beaten to its knees by Noël Coward and the young men he gathered around him to make a film which will surely triumph as entertainment wherever it is shown."

In the *New York Times* Bosley Crowther felt that "the great thing Mr. Coward has accomplished in the film is a full and complete expression of national fortitude" and quoted lines Kipling had written during the last war:

How in all times of our distress
And our deliverance too,
The game is more than the player of the game
And the ship is more than the crew.

But the words that undoubtedly brought a smile to the Coward lips came from American critic, Herb Sterne. The previous year had seen Orson Welles's cinematic *tour de force* as the writer-director-star of *Citizen Kane*. Sterne wrote: "He [Coward] might be described as the British Orson Welles, if Orson could write, act, direct, sing, dance, compose songs and be amusing."

Nor was the praise restricted to the professional critics. Brendan Bracken at the wartime Ministry of Information considered it "a rousing success" and "the greatest film ever made."

All the earlier disagreements were forgotten and now he was writing: "I hope you will consider very carefully my suggestion that you should make a film about the Army and am sure you could make one which would be as rousing a success as *In Which We Serve* . . . perhaps you will have time to think about this suggestion early next year."

(In fact, the "rousing" Army film was eventually made but not by Noël. Private correspondence reveals that Bracken and like-minded Army brass then switched their attention to Noël's old friend David Niven—possibly in the hope that he might be able to prevail upon Noël. And indeed, it's perfectly possible that he did act as a behind-the-scenes adviser to Niven on what emerged in 1944 as *The Way Ahead*—directed [ironically] by Carol Reed.)

Anthony Eden at the Foreign Office wrote to thank Noël for the film: "I was moved, proud and ashamed—proud of the Royal Navy, ashamed to be sitting at a desk myself and moved because I d....d well couldn't help being. You have created many and varied works of art. You have never done anything so big as this, so restrained, unselfish and inspired. No other living man could have done it."

But perhaps the most significant convert to the cause—and the one who gave Noël most personal pleasure—was Winston Churchill. Totally opposed to the project at the outset, he greatly admired the execution, saw the film several times and cheerfully admitted it brought tears to his eyes every time.

There was only one near-hiccup. The complex structure of the film involved some of the sea battles being shown out of sequence. When the fatal encounter is shown there is a caption indicating time and place—Crete 1941. After seeing the film a second time Churchill muttered to Mountbatten that he found it more confusing than he had remembered and asked Mountbatten to have a word with Coward about it.

Diplomat that he was, Mountbatten chose not to pass the word on until much later and then explained to Noël that, just before the caption came up, the Prime Minister had been called to the phone to receive the news that the Libyan counterattack had just begun. "I'm afraid he had other things on his mind," he added soothingly, and was later to repeat that the King himself had reprimanded Churchill for his lack of understanding.

Nor were the professional colleagues stinting in their praise.

Impresario Binkie Beaumont—who was to stage so many of Noël's West End plays—felt it was like seeing "a kind of magnificently gigantic News Reel . . . I really believe that I have been to sea and lived with the *Tryon*." He also put into words a perception shared by many: "If your career had been in Pictures all your life, surely it would have been amazing, but having only done *The Scoundrel* as an actor, there are no words."

From Hollywood a deeply moved Basil Rathbone wrote on behalf of the British expatriate community, promising to intensify their efforts to help the war effort. "The film," he wrote, "moved me more deeply than anything on celluloid has ever done before." From New York writer Alexander Woollcott— founder member of the famous Algonquin Round Table and an acerbic friend from Noël's first visits in the 1920s—began by cleverly parodying Elyot's

The Royal Family gave public support to the controversial project. Actor Bernard Miles (left) talks to the Duchess and Duke of Kent on the set.

speech from *Private Lives*—"There isn't a particle of you that I know, remember, or want . . ."—before sincerity overcame him: "but my hat is off to you . . . I've seen three or four good movies in my time. This is one of them."

Douglas Fairbanks, Jr.—also serving in the U.S. Navy—snatched a few hours shore leave to see the film and wrote: "The film was so honest that it hurt . . . I felt a chill of pride in the service itself and linked myself in with the cameraderie of the sea. I experienced a new, strange sort of 'service' patriotism—a gladness that we are all fighting together for the same kind of people in the same kind of world."

He recalled the moments in the film that had stuck in his mind:

> I want to hear Celia Johnson's toast again—Capt. "D's" farewell to his men—Joyce Carey before the blitz—Johnny Mills' remark on Chamberlain's declaration of war—the look on the lad's face as he left his post of duty—the two lovers walking round the horse-dung in the road—Bernard Miles all the time—the day on the downs with the dog-fight overhead—oh, so many things . . . Your construction, dialogue, dramatic inflections and punctuation showed a thorough knowledge of what was meant when the words "Motion Pictures" were coined . . . all of us, belonging primarily to films, are enriched by having such a giant join our ranks.

The circle was completed when he received a letter from Mountbatten himself, now at Combined Operations: "I would never have believed," Mountbatten wrote, "that one could get such different shades of opinion in the Navy to be so unanimous on any subject, let alone a film! . . . What a terrific triumph all this is for you!" In the P.S. he listed his only critical comments—which have a slightly ironical ring to them, since he supposedly didn't want the *Tryon* identified with the *Kelly*! "I tried hard to find some faults with the picture and, but for the regrettable fact that you made the *Tryon* capsize to starboard, whereas the *Kelly* capsized to port, I could find no technical inaccuracy. I would have preferred you not to have given the order 'Abandon ship,' as I had always said this was an order we would exclude from the *Kelly* . . . However, what a minute point this is and one hardly worth mentioning."

* * * *

Even though the film did not qualify for the Hollywood Oscars, as the rules were presently framed, the Academy made a special award in 1943 to Noël for his "outstanding production achievement" on the film. When he saw it again towards the end of his life, he was "the first to admit (it) is a rattling good movie. I wept steadily throughout."

* * * *

The film's success prompted several abortive postscripts.

Del Giudice's career prospered for a while—particularly with courageous productions such as Olivier's *Henry V* (1944) and *Hamlet* (1948)—but his extravagance was soon out of keeping with the post war austerity that gripped the British film industry and by the end of the decade he had been sidelined. In later years *In Which We Serve* came to have a somewhat talismanic quality for him. Noël's correspondence files show him writing on a number of occasions with one proposition or another, all of which required Noël's personal endorsement or financial subsidy and occasionally both. The two men did not work together again. Del Giudice died in 1961.

In late 1941, while the film was in active preparation, there was a suggestion that Noël should write "a German *Cavalcade*." Robert Vansittart (for whom Noël was then working) was approached at the Ministry by a Mrs. Giffard-Young and passed the suggestion on to Noël. The idea was to create a storyline which would incidentally trace the evolution of German society to demonstrate how it had reached its present crisis. There is some evidence that Clemence Dane—Noël's old friend and early collaborator in the *White Ensign* days—started to rough out a treatment involving a children's governess visiting Germany before the project was aborted. There is none that Noël himself ever took it seriously enough to put pen to paper. In any case, he was otherwise deeply engaged in the propaganda war.

As if Vansittart hadn't enough to do, he found himself bombarded with letters from Mrs. Giffard-Young (and subsequently her agent) with claims for both creative and financial credit for the idea, once it was executed. Finally, he had an aide wire back to say: "Lord Vansittart is not an agent for 'steering ideas' into Mr. Noël Coward's ports. Mr. Noël Coward is quite capable of building his own ships and is, moreover, not wholly inexperienced as a harbour master."

Mrs. Giffard-Young was not heard from again and Clemence Dane turned to a life of Frederick the Great.

* * * *

There was to be one other small film commitment connected to the war years and one which only surfaced in researching material for the Coward Centenary film retrospectives.

A French documentary was made in 1945 detailing the story of the French Resistance in Paris. Under the title *Journal de la Résistance* it is believed by some scholars to have been the work of Jean Grémillon (1902–1959). The thirty-five-minute script is credited to one Pierre Blanchard and in the English language version the narration is read by Coward. Blanchard wrote to him from the Office Français d'Information Cinématographique: "Votre commentarie est merveilleux . . . votre collaboration est inéstimable—vous n'avez considéré que l'apport moral qu'elle representait mais il faut que vous sachez aussi que le produit de l'exploration du *Journal de la Résistance* est dévolu aux familles des F.F.I. tués at aux blessés de l'insurrection. . . . un bienfait matériel infiniment touchant."

* * * *

Perhaps the most fitting finale, though, was this one. Noël was lunching with his three collaborators and discussing plans for future projects. At the next table, quite oblivious of their neighbours, a couple began to discuss the film and Noël's performance in particular—of which they were quite critical. Noël was the first to leave. On his way out of the restaurant he paused before the offending table and said, loudly and distinctly—"*I* thought I was *very* good."

THIS HAPPY BREED (1943)

The play was written in 1939, produced in 1943 at the Haymarket Theatre, London, where it alternated with *Present Laughter*.

PLAY SYNOPSIS

It's 1919 and Frank and Ethel Gibbons are moving into their new house in Clapham Common. The Gibbons family consists of three children—Reg, Queenie and Vi—Frank's hypochondriac sister, Ethel, and his mother-in-law, Mrs. Flint. After four years of war, they have a home of their own at last. The first person they meet is a helpful neighbour, Bob Mitchell, who Frank recognises as a wartime comrade in arms.

Six years later and the children are grown. Christmas lunch is over and the young ones have the dining room to themselves. Reg, the eldest, has his friend, Sam Leadbitter, a young Communist he idolises, rather to the consternation of his parents. Queenie, the elder of the two girls, is turning into a rather flighty miss. When Billy Mitchell, Bob's sailor son, comes in on his way back to his ship and proposes to her, she refuses him. She wants the kind of good life he can never afford.

It's 1926 now and the General Strike has just ended. The women are sitting at the supper table. For once Ethel is impatient with her mother's endless complaints. She is worried about Reg, who has been away for days and in the thick of the demonstrations with Sam. Phyllis, Reg's girlfriend, arrives, equally concerned—followed by Frank and Bob, who have been volunteer bus drivers during the strike, now slightly inebriated. Soon after Reg and Sam arrive. Reg has been slightly hurt. Vi gives Sam a piece of her mind and tells him he needn't come courting her any more. Left alone with his son, Frank has a man-to-man chat for the first time. Everyone has a right to his ideas, he explains, but make them *your* ideas—not someone else's secondhand versions like Sam's, which have never worked and won't now. The old country's tired after the war but it's up to ordinary people like them to keep things steady.

Another five years have passed and everyone is looking that much older. It's the day of Reg's wedding to Phyllis and the Gibbons's household is in chaos. Bob Mitchell arrives and we learn that his wife is now an invalid and that Sam has married Vi and given up revolutions. Billy drops in—now a petty officer—and runs into Queenie in her bridesmaid dress. She has just turned him down again and admitted to him that she is involved with a married man. Ethel and Frank come down in their wedding finery, only to be told by a distraught Queenie that she wants to get away from their petty suburban life. Frank tells her sharply that "there are worse things than being ordinary and respectable" and that, while she is in his house, she will behave. As they wait for the cars to take them to the wedding, all the family tensions are on view but, once they arrive, a united family leaves for the church.

A month later. In the early hours Queenie creeps downstairs, suitcase in hand. She puts a note on the mantelpiece and leaves. Soon after, Frank and Bob come in from a regimental reunion feeling no pain and determined to

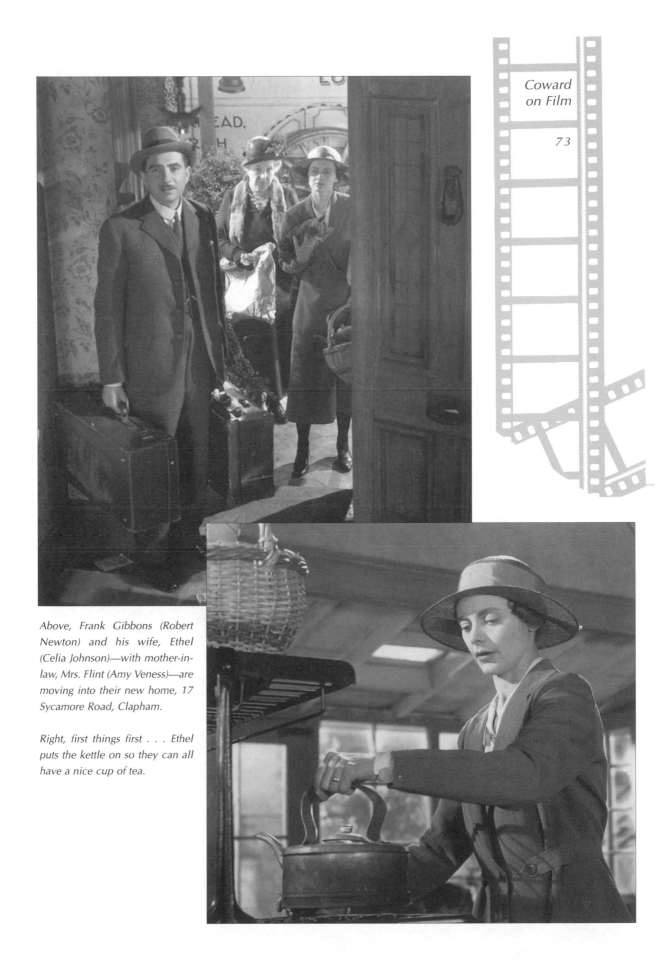

Above, Frank Gibbons (Robert Newton) and his wife, Ethel (Celia Johnson)—with mother-in-law, Mrs. Flint (Amy Veness)—are moving into their new home, 17 Sycamore Road, Clapham.

Right, first things first . . . Ethel puts the kettle on so they can all have a nice cup of tea.

have "one for the road." As they sit and chat, they discuss their kids. Frank wishes Queenie would settle down and marry Billy. They reminisce about the war and wonder about the next one. The one for the road proves to be their undoing. They drop the bottle and the noise wakes Ethel. Bob leaves hurriedly and then they find Queenie's note. Frank wants to find her and bring her back but Ethel will have none of it. Queenie is no longer any daughter of hers. She will never take her back.

1932. Mrs. Flint and Sylvia are chatting. Sylvia has given up hypochondria for Christian Science. She remarks that she has noticed a letter to Frank from Queenie. Ethel enters and asks them not to mention the girl's name. Later she apologises for her outburst but she has had a presentiment of bad luck. Suddenly Vi arrives with the news that Reg and Phyllis have been killed in a car accident. Frank and Ethel are left alone, sitting quietly, hand in hand.

The night of the Abdication—December 10, 1936. The family is gathered round the radio to hear the King's farewell speech. They are interrupted by the arrival of Billy Mitchell, who brings them news of their daughter. She has been abandoned by her lover and managing on the Continent as best she could. Ethel asks where she is now and Billy tells her that Queenie Mitchell—now his wife—is waiting next door with his father. Will she be welcome? After so many years mother and daughter are reunited.

September 30, 1938. Mrs. Flint and Bob's wife have "passed on." Frank comes in, upset to sense the mood of the crowds in the street, "yelling themselves hoarse without the faintest idea what they're yelling about." Having

Billy Mitchell (John Mills), Bob's son, has always loved Queenie (Kay Walsh), though she thinks herself too good for him. Undeterred, he later finds her down on her luck, marries her, and brings her home.

fought in the last war, he does not believe Chamberlain's appeasement is the answer this time. Billy is in Singapore and Queenie is to join him, leaving their baby son in the care of Frank and Ethel until she settles. Bob Mitchell is leaving his house next door and comes in for a farewell drink. He and Frank talk over all that has happened in the years they have been neighbours and Frank wonders whether houses that have been lived in so long keep memories of the people who lived there.

June 1939—just twenty years since the Gibbons moved in and now they are moving out and into a new flat. The family are all gone and now there are just the two of them—and, of course, their grandson. While Ethel prepares the final meal, Frank rocks the baby's pram and confides to this next generation his feelings about life and the future. This country of theirs has gone through some tough times lately but the people will pull her through. They've fought hard to keep the values they believe in for centuries and they'll fight fifty wars, if they have to.

Ethel finds him talking and brings him in to supper.

* * * *

The film version was made in 1943 in Technicolor by Cineguild for Two Cites and was first shown in London at the Gaumont, Haymarket, and the Marble Arch Pavilion simultaneously on May 29, 1944.

CREDITS

Producers	Noël Coward (Anthony Havelock-Allan)
Director	David Lean
Screenplay	David Lean, Ronald Neame and Anthony Havelock-Allan
Photography	Ronald Neame
Editor	Jack Harris
Music	Noël Coward
Art Director to Noël Coward	Gladys Calthrop

CAST

Frank Gibbons	Robert Newton
Ethel Gibbons	Celia Johnson
Billy Mitchell	John Mills
Queenie Gibbons	Kay Walsh
Bob Mitchell	Stanley Holloway
Mrs. Flint	Amy Veness
Aunt Sylvia	Alison Leggatt
Vi	Eileen Erskine
Reg	John Blythe
Sam Leadbetter	Guy Verney
Edie	Merle Tottenham
Phyllis	Betty Fleetwood
Narrator	Laurence Olivier

This Happy Breed can easily be seen as a semi-sequel to *Cavalcade* with the Gibbons as middle class Marryots. It covers the life of one family plus their neighbours from 1919 to 1939. That aside, it has significant differences from the earlier piece. On the one hand, it lacks the social and class conflicts that underpinned *Cavalcade*, since it concentrates almost entirely on lower middle class people and values.

On the other, the period it depicts—as seen at the time of writing (1939)—was altogether more edgy than its predecessor. In 1930, when *Cavalcade* was written, it was possible to see events like the Boer War, the sinking of the *Titanic*, even World War I as history. A decade later the Depression, the threat of Communism and the certainty of another "war to end wars" were all too close and uncomfortable. In 1930 it was possible to look forward; there was no such luxury available in 1939.

The resemblances to *In Which We Serve* are obvious in the domestic scenes. The home lives of the Hardys and the Blakes in that film are virtually interchangeable with that of the Gibbons with their sibling squabbling and crotchety in-laws. Or perhaps one should say *vice versa*, since *This Happy Breed* was written first.

Not surprisingly, given the national mood of the times, both share the same attitude towards the grim prospects for the future. No matter how bad things get, Britain can take it and will once again muddle through. As Frank tells his grandson, "The people themselves, the ordinary people like you and me, we know what we belong to, where we come from, and where we're going. We may not know it with our brains, but we know it with our roots."

Noël enjoyed writing about ordinary people and took London pride in it, but reactions to this aspect of his talent were often equivocal. Graham Greene—a film critic at the time—was distinctly critical and not for the first time. "Mr. Coward," he considered, "was separated from ordinary life by his theatrical success and one suspects that when he does overhear the common speech he finds himself overwhelmed by the pathos of its very cheapness and inadequacy. But it is the sense of inadequacy he fails to convey, and with it he loses the pathos." Dilys Powell echoed the thought: "Should not the observation be a trifle less benevolent, the defence of the ordinary man a trifle less condescending?"

Noël himself had more than an inkling of the problem, as far as *This Happy Breed* was concerned.

He wrote of the original play—and by implication the film, too, "the character of Frank Gibbons is a fraction more than life-size. His views are too clearly expressed to be quite true to life. I have no doubt whatsoever that he would hold such views, but, to my mind, his articulateness throughout the play concedes too much to theatrical effectiveness. Had he been a character in a novel, this error could have been eliminated; the author could have explained his feelings and reactions without imposing upon him the burden of speaking them aloud. However, *This Happy Breed* was a play written for the theatre and must stand or fall within the theatre's necessary limitations."

His reservations were shared by Robert Donat, Noël's first choice to play Frank. He wrote to Noël in April 1942 that he found the play "thick with atmosphere" and complimented him on his "great gift for conveying essen-

tial detail in a line or two" which "gives us a sense of depth and size far beyond the limits of the room we see." He went on to wonder, however, "if the time for the play was not past."

> Right at the end I don't believe in the things that Frank believes in. He's human and lovable and, above all, he's adult and I like him enormously—until he tries to justify himself and his kind; then I'm mad with him. Rightly or wrongly, I believe it is just that very political irresponsibility that got us into another war. I don't believe he does know 'what we belong to, where we come from, and where we're going.' Until we *do* know it, with our brains and hearts and souls as well as our roots, we shall go on fighting these bloody wars.

But, then, he concludes, apologetically refusing the offer, "I'm only a bloody actor. I'm immensely proud that you even thought of me." The part went to Robert Newton.

In the film version Frank's philosophical final speech to his grandson was omitted. David Lean persuaded Noël that, much as he liked it theatrically— it was the companion piece to *Cavalcade's* "Toast to the Future"—it simply would not work on film. Reluctantly, Noël first trimmed, then finally conceded and cut it.

By and large *This Happy Breed* opts for retaining the stage effects but when director David Lean does decide to embellish, it's possible to see what he might have made of a freer screenplay which did not come with stage history attached.

Comrades-in-arms. Frank finds that their nextdoor neighbour is none other than his old wartime companion Bob Mitchell (Stanley Holloway).

For instance, Frank's "father's chat" to Reg before the wedding was necessarily set in the single parlour set in the original but in the film it takes place in the lavatory, neatly underscoring the awkwardness of the moment and the pomposity of an embarrassed father's words.

Later a trip to the cinema—a device to be used again in *Brief Encounter*—contrasts contemporary social values with those of other places. The film is *Broadway Melody* (1929), an early "talkies" musical. ("You know, I don't understand a word they say," a member of the audience is heard to remark.) And a small detail—Ethel's taking down of King Edward's calendar after the Abdication—can be telling when observed intimately on film but overstated when it becomes the whole focus of what is happening on stage.

Apart from the visit to the cinema, the film is "opened out" to involve the family with other events of the period, as when they visit the Wembley Exhibition of 1924 or when we see Frank and neighbour Bob Mitchell driving a bus during the General Strike.

For the first time Lean uses the camera as a character. On three specific occasions it suggests a mood or point of view without the need for any of the characters to articulate it. The first—devised by Ronald Neame—occurs when daughter Vi comes in to break the news of Reg's death. First she tells her grandmother and aunt, who leave the room. Then, when Vi goes to find her parents in the garden, the camera remains and examines the empty room. When Frank and Ethel slowly enter, it then retreats to observe them from a respectful distance, much as a visitor would. Later, when Queenie leaves home, the camera pulls back outside the house, leaving Frank and Ethel imprisoned, as the rain beats down.

The device of camera-as-commentator is repeated at the very end of the film, when Frank and Ethel leave their home for the last time. As they close the front door, the camera stays inside the house, drifting up the stairs and taking a last look round the empty rooms—very much as it had moved down to welcome the newcomers in the film's opening shot. Finally, on a dissolve, from high above, we see the row of identical houses that is Sycamore Road, in one of which (No. 17) we have been privileged to live for the last twenty years. On the soundtrack we hear "London Pride."

Lean's handling of character showed a marked advance from his previous film and in later years he was generous in his appreciation of what he had learned from Noël. "You've got to know what every character eats for breakfast," Noël told him, "even though you should never show them eating breakfast. You've got to know what sort of people they are. Would they do this or that? It's a question of taste with characters, it's like knowing a living human being. Once you understand this, you know what you want from the actors, and as most of them are very good, working with them is not difficult."

*   *   *   *

Pleased with the results of their collaboration on *In Which We Serve*, Noël agreed to let David Lean be the sole director on any future collaborations—of which *This Happy Breed* was the first. (Lean wrote to Noël to express his appreciation of "your generosity and faith in giving me *Happy Breed* all on my lonesome, and hope to God I won't let your writing down. I assure you I will do my very best.")

The film also marked the debut of a new production company, Cineguild, formed by Lean, cameraman Ronald Neame and producer Anthony Havelock-Allan and named in emulation of the famous American Theatre Guild. Like most other independents, it operated under the umbrella of a "parent" company (Independent Producers) with its productions financed and distributed by the J. Arthur Rank Organisation.

The trio was responsible for the screenplay, which remained faithful to the original text. "When there was new dialogue required, Havelock-Allan recalled, "Noël wrote it."

Noël himself found it "pleasant to be concerned with the picture but not trapped by it" and felt the film was "on the whole very well done. Celia Johnson, Kay Walsh, Johnnie Mills and Stanley Holloway were first rate, and the Technicolor, after much discussion, was reduced to its minimum, delicately balanced and for once did not sear the eyeballs with oleographic oranges and reds and yellows." At that time there were only four Technicolor cameras in England.

What he neglected to note was that he had initially wanted to play the part of Frank Gibbons himself. He had, after all, written the part for himself and he was currently playing it, first on tour and then in the West End. It took a great deal of courage on David Lean's part—even after the success of *In Which We*

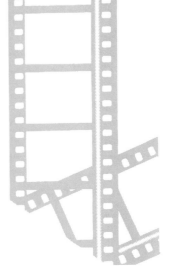

Direct David Lean (right) supervises the Armistice Day parade in one of the scenes Lean uses to "open up" the stage action.

Serve—to dissuade him and equal professional discipline on Noël's part to defer to his director's judgement on the matter. (It was ironic that Lean should continue to feel so strongly—"Noël Coward playing a lower middle-class man? . . . I saw it on the stage with Noël and he *just* about got away with it but, really, not good . . ."—considering Noël had been born into just such a background. He was, of course, to play Frank in the 1956 U.S. TV version.) He was shrewd enough to realise that what seemed to work on stage might come off very differently on screen. Noël finally agreed with some reluctance to Lean giving the part to the alcoholically unpredictable Robert Newton.

By remaining remarkably faithful to the original, the film was hugely popular with contemporary cinema audiences, who made it one of the most successful at the 1944 box office. It cost £220,000.

In the *Observer* C. A. Lejeune compared it favourably with *In Which We Serve*, a film she had much admired: "It is a deliberate study of the lives of an ordinary suburban family in the flat years between the two wars, and the trouble with any honest study of ordinary people is that ordinary tends to seem a little ordinary. The special talent of *This Happy Breed* is so quiet that it hardly becomes manifest. It appears to record drab, physical facts from the outside, while actually indicating a mute spiritual experience from within."

Another critic, who obviously knew his Coward: "This bitter sweet family album of the private lives of people with no design for living is too much a conversation piece to make a perfectly satisfactory film, amusing and moving though it is." But most critics agreed with Lejeune that the film transcended its apparent triviality of subject. The *Manchester Guardian* called it "an essential 'photo' for John Bull's family album."

Havelock-Allan wrote to Noël that he was relieved to see that "nobody seems to have rumbled Bobby Newton" and that the majority of the critics had had "the grace to like his performance less than those of the other principals."

All of them agreed on the performance of Celia Johnson—already and still in the minds of most people the definitive Coward film actress. In Lejeune's words:

> [T]here is one magnificent performance. Celia Johnson plays the wife, the drably named Ethel Gibbons. She plays her in drab silk blouses, drab skirts, drab hair, and sometimes a fierce Technicolor makeup. Often she looks awful, but by thunder! as an actress she's superb. The wife with diplomatic relations to preserve between husband and family. The mother of a son, lost in thoughts of her lost son; the mother of a daughter, harshly tender with the daughter; the grandmother, ardent but a little tired, heavily applying herself to the cares of a younger woman; there are not many actresses of Miss Johnson's age who could even begin to rough out this manifold personality . . . This is beautiful acting; the sort of acting the French have been taught to understand; confessional acting from the inside outwards.

Johnson herself was able to see herself more pragmatically: "I look so awful that even the friend who came with me . . . couldn't say anything but that I was meant to look very drab and certainly succeeded."

By this time Johnson was gaining something of a reputation among film crews for her total concentration. Because she had young children to get home to and because "home" was a long way from the studio, she had special dispensation to catch a particular train on Saturdays. Filming was running late when Lean decided he wanted to try a take of the difficult emotional scene where Queenie returns home, uncertain of the reception she'll receive from her mother. Would Celia try it just once? Looking at her watch, she decided that she had five minutes. Three minutes later the take was "in the can," and many of the crew were in tears through the emotion she had radiated. At which point Johnson looked at her watch again. "Can I go now, please?"

* * * *

Although Noël did not adapt the play himself for the film version, he was made aware of the problems subsequently when he prepared the material for the live television production he did for CBS in 1956. Cutting to fit the programme length—ninety minutes minus commercials—was a problem and, of course, the setting was an unfamiliar one to American TV viewers (" . . . in order to frame it, I have written an introduction explaining the play, and I shall speak the introduction as myself on film.")

This Happy Breed was, in fact, a second choice. Noël's original intention had been to produce a TV version of *Present Laughter* with Claudette Colbert as Liz but the reaction of the sponsors to some of the lines in the earlier *Blithe Spirit* caused William Paley, the head of CBS, to lose his nerve over the project. *Present Laughter*, he felt, might be too much for the sensibilities of middle America. Having first postponed it, he eventually plucked up the courage to cancel it.

By this time, Noël had already finished the TV adaptation, which he had retitled *Twinkle, Twinkle, Little Star*. He records the process in his *Diary*:

> <u>February 19th, 1956</u>
>
> I sprang at (it) like a surgeon and carved an hour and ten minutes out of it without, I think, impairing its essential quality. There was a moment, I admit, when I strode up and down the room quivering with panic and despair crying, "I can't! I can't! It's no good going on, the play is too tightly constructed to whittle down to an hour and twenty minutes, and by eliminating the majority of its sex implications, so that millions of Bible-thumping, puritanical, asinine televiewers should not have their outraged sensibilities outraged, I shall emasculate the whole thing and have nothing left but a febrile shambles of mangled witticisms." However, I wriggled my way out of this Slough of Despond and pressed on valiantly, and now it is done . . . This cutting of my plays down for television is certainly a salutary experience, and I believe the next time I embark on a full-length play for the theatre, I shall find I have profited by it. I shall have learned, for instance, to dispense with amusing irrelevancies that have no direct bearing on the story and to get back to my original method of saying what I have to say in as few lines as possible with a minimum of atmospheric padding and linguistic flourishes.

Then came the switch . . .

The TV version was produced live in colour in New York and was sponsored by the "Ford Star Jubilee" through the J. Walter Thompson advertising agency. It was broadcast on May 5, 1956.

CAST

Mrs. Flint	Norah Howard
Ethel	Edna Best
Sylvia	Beulah Garrick
Frank Gibbons	Noël Coward
Bob Mitchell	Guy S. Paull
Reg	Robert Chapman
Queenie	Patricia Cutts
Vi	Joy Ash
Sam Leadbitter	Rhoderick Walker
Phyllis Blake	Sally Pierce
Edie	Vera Marshall
Billy	Roger Moore

*   *   *   *

His first exposure to live TV drama did little to encourage him: "I'm impressed not with the amount of brains but of brawn which handles the amazing technical achievements. But the brains is coming up."

From the *Diary* of May 6:

> Well, it is all over . . . Last night, before the credits were over on the screen, CBS had over a thousand telephone calls. Bill Paley called me immediately and told me it was the greatest thing he has ever seen on television. His voice was still husky with emotion . . . Apparently I gave a really fine performance, a great deal of which I owe to Edna, who was magnificent. She was calm and sure and infinitely touching . . . It is so lovely for her after those dreadful months of mental misery in the clinic to come back like this and she has been so ideal all through rehearsals that I am forever in her debt. [Edna Best was making her comeback in this taxing part after a long absence.] The rapport between us was so strong that it gave the play a little personal magic that it has never had before either on the stage or the screen.

A week later he could confirm that "the notices have been fabulous. The New York ones soberly enthusiastic and most heart-warming but they were nothing compared with the raves from Philadelphia, Chicago, Detroit, Los Angeles, San Francisco, etc. The general consensus of opinion is that *This Happy Breed* is the finest telecast ever done and my performance the best of all!"

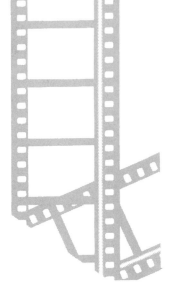

BLITHE SPIRIT (1945)

The play was written in 1941 and produced at the Piccadilly Theatre, London, on July 21, 1941, subsequently transferring to the Duchess Theatre. In all it ran for 1,997 performances, a record at the time.

PLAY SYNOPSIS

The play is set in the home of Charles and Ruth Condomine. Charles is a writer and he has invited Madame Arcati, a medium, to join them for dinner that evening, so that he can research his next book. Ruth is his second wife and while they wait for their guests, Charles is reminiscing about Elvira, his first and late wife. While the subject doesn't exactly please Ruth, having been married before, she knows how to be tolerant.

The American poster. Not precisely what The Master had in mind!

Madame Arcati (Margaret Rutherford) appears to see an optimistic outcome. By now Charles and Ruth would give a great deal to share it.

The first guests arrive—Dr. Bradman and his wife—and the four of them discuss the evening ahead. All of them are sceptical about the séance. Madame Arcati arrives—an eccentric and bizarrely-dressed woman, totally confident of her otherworldly powers.

Dinner over, they settle down to the business in hand. Madam Arcati explains about her "control" child "on the other side" called Daphne. She puts on a record of the song "Always" (Daphne's favourite) and turns off the lights. The table begins to move and Madame Arcati announces that someone wishes to speak to Charles. She then goes into a trance and some force overturns the table. Amid the consternation a woman's voice, heard only by Charles, introduces herself as Elvira. Charles manages to pass this off as Madame Arcati recovers and leaves, claiming she has felt a presence in the room.

The Bradmans leave and Charles and Ruth are preparing to enjoy a nightcap when Charles catches sight of Elvira. Since Ruth can't see her, the conversation that follows is not without ambiguities. Finally, Ruth—upset by what she considers Charles's inebriated ramblings—goes off to bed in a huff, leaving Charles and Elvira alone.

Elvira herself is upset not to be more warmly welcomed, having been sent for. When asked who sent for her, she replies that it was that awful adenoidal spirit child, Daphne. What's more, she doesn't know how to go back.

At breakfast the next morning Ruth hasn't entirely forgiven Charles for his behaviour. Elvira appears and the same kind of one-sided conversation resumes. By this time Ruth believes that her husband is becoming deranged and tries to humour him, but when Charles makes Elvira demonstrate her (still unseen) presence, Ruth goes into hysterics.

Ruth now consults Madame Arcati, who is thrilled at what she considers to be a professional success. However, when Ruth demands the medium exorcise Elvira and finds she cannot, there is a row, which ends with Madame Arcati leaving. Charles enters with Elvira and a three-way conversation ensues in which the women fight over Charles. Elvira is secretly pleased that Madame Arcati can't send her back but Ruth vows to stop at nothing. She storms out and Charles goes off to calm her, leaving Elvira alone. Edith, the maid, enters the room to find a gramophone playing "Always" and some unseen force replacing the record every time she removes it. She leaves in terror.

Mrs. Bradman is sympathising with Ruth over the spate of accidents that seem to be happening in the Condomine household. Edith has fallen down stairs and Charles has sprained his arm. Ruth knows very well that Elvira is the cause. Charles enters with Dr. Bradman, who is concerned about his mental state, but Ruth explains that he is often this way when working on a new book. Charles declares his intention to drive into the nearby town. At this, Elvira who has accompanied him, unseen by the others, quickly leaves the room.

After the Bradmans leave, Ruth tells Charles that she is convinced Elvira intends to kill him, so that she can have him to herself "on the other side." Charles poo-poohs the idea but Ruth leaves to drive over and consult Madame Arcati. No sooner has she left than Elvira returns. She wants Charles to take her on an outing to the cinema and when he explains that they can't possibly go until Ruth returns with the car, she becomes frantic. Charles immediately realises that she has tampered with the car and at that moment he receives the news that Ruth has crashed and been killed. Suddenly the door bursts open and Elvira is attacked by an unseen Ruth, while Charles looks on, appalled at this latest turn of events.

A few days later Madame Arcati visits Charles. She thinks she might have found a way to dematerialise spirits, if he would be interested. He would be more interested than she can imagine. Elvira enters and Charles introduces her to the enthusiastic medium, even if she is invisible. Elvira asks to speak to Charles alone and tells him that she wants to go back. Madame Arcati attempts an exorcism— which only results in Ruth materialising. He now has *two* ghostly ex-wives!

Several hours later and all Madame Arcati's spells have been tried in vain. Everyone is exhausted. Madame Arcati is convinced that someone in the house summoned up Elvira and only that person can release her spirit. In her crystal she sees a white bandage and invokes Edith, the maid, who is wearing a bandage because of her accident. It becomes clear to all of them that she can see the spirits and must be the medium through whom they materialised. Madame Arcati puts the girl into a trance and manages to send both women back.

Advising Charles to move away from these surroundings, Madame Arcati leaves. Charles packs up and talks to his ex and absent wives, telling them that he is going out of the reach of both of them. He also tells them what he really thinks of them. There is an immediate outburst of poltergeist activity with objects being thrown and the room being destroyed around him, as he manages to escape.

*The séance. The shadow of medium Madame Arcati looms over the sceptical foursome—
Mrs. Bradman (Joyce Carey), Charles, Dr. Bradman (Hugh Wakefield), and Ruth.*

The film version was made in Technicolor by Cineguild for Two Cities in 1944/5 and first shown at the Odeon, Leicester Square, in April 1945.

CREDITS

Producer	Noël Coward (Anthony Havelock-Allan)
Director	David Lean
Screenplay	David Lean, Ronald Neame and Anthony Havelock-Allan
Photography	Ronald Neame
Editor	Jack Harris
Incidental Music	Richard Addinsell
Art Director	C. P. Norman
Art Supervisor to Noël Coward	Gladys Calthrop

CAST

Charles Condomine	Rex Harrison
Ruth Condomine	Constance Cummings
Elvira	Kay Hammond
Madame Arcati	Margaret Rutherford
Dr. Bradman	Hugh Wakefield
Mrs. Bradman	Joyce Carey
Edith	Jacqueline Clark

* * * *

The film opens with an embellishment. Over a background of Victorian sampler designs, Noël's voice reads a preface new to the play and perhaps a retrospective view of what it was really about:

When we are young
We read and believe
The most fantastic things.
When we grow older and wiser
We learn with perhaps a little regret
That these things can never be.

The "little regret" was reflected in the film itself and Noël's own verdict seemed to encapsulate most people's opinion of the film: "I will draw a light, spangled veil over *Blithe Spirit*. It wasn't entirely bad but it was a great deal less good than it should have been."

Anyone who enjoyed the play would have enjoyed the film—which in view of the play's phenomenal London run—exceeded even today only by *The Mousetrap*—gave it a considerable potential audience. To guarantee a smooth transition from stage to screen, Kay Hammond and Margaret Rutherford repeated their roles of Elvira and Madame Arcati.

If any further insurance was required, the popularity of the three "Topper" films in the 1930s—based on Thorne Smith's characters—would seem to indicate that amusing ghosts made good box office.

Margaret Rutherford, Kay Hammond, and Rex Harrison pose for a production still.

Casting, however, provided several problems which no one had expected. While Margaret Rutherford bumbled effortlessly from one happy medium to the next, scarcely seeming to notice the change, the two wives didn't create the kind of chemistry the play demanded. Ethereal on the stage, Kay Hammond (Elvira) did not photograph well. Constance Cummings (Ruth) did. This was brought home to David Lean when he overheard one of the crew observe—after Ruth had stormed off to bed, leaving Charles to the devices of the ghostly Elvira—that he personally wouldn't hang around with her when he had the other one waiting upstairs for him!

But, as it turned out, the principal piece of miscasting was Rex Harrison. Irritated initially to be dragged out of his military service before the war was over to star in the film—a release he presciently attributed to the influence of Noël and his friend Mountbatten—he soon found himself at odds with several important aspects of the project.

In the first place he was one of the few people who didn't like the original play. In his autobiography he persists in referring to it as *Blythe Spirit*. In the second he did not believe that his director had a sense of humour. In that he was wrong, but he was correct insofar as their respective styles were incompatible and he did not know at the time that Lean—who was also no fan of the play—had suggested to Noël that he was not ready to direct light comedy. Noël laughingly dismissed Lean's protestations, pressed the button, and the project was under way.

As proof of Lean's limitations, Harrison subsequently complained that he did nothing more than set up a stage set and photograph it: "Four of us got up in line and then Margaret Rutherford would walk down the middle pulling faces."

While there may have been a strong element of the "camera-in-the-stalls" about Lean's direction of the film, the real problem was Harrison himself. At thirty-six (and looking younger) and for all his technique, he could not portray the character Noël intended Charles to be—a middle aged man with his wild oats safely sown, who wants nothing but a quiet life, not the excitement of a big-amous marriage that Harrison's Charles seems to anticipate. In addition, Harrison placed a high value on his screen "charm"; he liked to be liked. Yet much of the play's humour derives from the discomfiture of a pompous, middle aged, rather unlikeable man. None of these qualities did Rex Harrison associate with the persona of "Rex Harrison" and he played the part accordingly.

*   *   *   *

What is disappointing after *In Which We Serve* and *This Happy Breed* is the lack of directorial presence. David Lean seems content to point his camera at the stage play and let the actors do the rest. There is a certain amount of "opening up"—a couple of scenes take place in Madame Arcati's cottage, we go for a car ride in which an invisible Elvira drives Charles, much to the consternation of an RAC patrolman on traffic duty; there is one inspired moment where we see Madame Arcati riding her bicycle with gay abandon through the Kentish lanes. What is missing is a point of view. All the characters are observed objectively and equally.

To be sure, there are occasional touches . . . Madame Arcati's spooky shadow on the wall as she prances into her trance can be interpreted as a satirical comment on the genre and on people who jump at shadows; likewise the montage of her exorcist paraphernalia. Lean repeats his juxtapositions, as when Madame Arcati's remark about noise upsetting her "vibrations" is immediately followed by a whistling kettle, the parrot muttering "Pretty Poltergeist" and so on. After the visual promise of the two previous films, however, the disappointment lies in the fact that one was expecting more.

In *This Happy Breed* Lean turned the house into an additional character. Using a multi-roomed set, he could free his camera to wander and by the end of the film we felt we knew the house—had even lived there. Even though he did the same and we are allowed to visit several different rooms in the Condomines' house and are frequently shown it from the outside, the feeling of a stage set persists. It's almost as if Lean were saying, "This piece is what it is, near perfect of its mannered kind. I shall capture it on film but I shall not tamper with it." One critic called it "a permanently frozen daiquiri."

The house, incidentally, was closely modeled on Goldenhurst, Noël's Kent country retreat. In case there is any doubt, we are shown a signpost at one point indicating "Ashford 8 miles."

The one significant divergence from the play is the ending. Instead of Charles beating a hasty retreat from ghostly retribution, he also dies and goes to meet his late wives in the "echoing vaults of eternity." The film ends with the three of them sitting on the garden wall wondering what to do next.

The plot change had little to do with any of the adaptors feeling that this would make a better or more dramatic *dénouement* and a great deal to do with the requirements of the film industry's production code. Unorthodox morals had to be seen to be punished and consigning these three essentially unpleasant people to eternal companionship seems sufficient justice.

While the film was in preparation Noël was out of the country and thus unable to exercise his normal prerogative of watching the daily rushes. He left with the crisp instruction to "Just photograph it" and saw nothing until the final film. At the end of the screening with his three "darlings," he was asked by David Lean for his opinion. "Well, dears," he is supposed to have said, "you've just fucked up the best thing I ever wrote."

When Lean reminded him that he had never claimed to be able to direct high comedy and did Noël have any other suggestions, Noël replied, "My dear, I think we'd better go back to a bit of real life." The "real life" was to be an adaptation of "Still Life," later known as *Brief Encounter*.

The critics, fortunately, didn't see it that way. William Whitebait in the *New Statesman* (not always a Coward *aficionado*) dubbed it "the wittiest, funniest creation of the English screen," C. A. Lejeune called it "ninety minutes of concentrated, cultivated fun," while in the *Daily Mail* Simon Harcourt-Smith considered it "a British comedy that, I think, surpasses the most competent and effervescent nonsense we have got from Hollywood in many a long year."

However, at the last count the film had yet to make its money back.

* * * *

In the 1950s Noël was asked to direct a ninety-minute TV production as part of a three programme contract with CBS. The first broadcast had been the extended duet with Mary Martin (*Together with Music*, 1955), and the third would turn out to be *This Happy Breed*.

The show went out live and in colour on January 14, 1956, from Hollywood with the following cast:

Charles Condomine	Noël Coward
Ruth Condomine	Claudette Colbert
Madame Arcati	Mildred Natwick
Elvira	Lauren Bacall
Dr. Bradman	Philip Tonge
Mrs. Bradman	Brenda Forbes
Edith	Marion Ross

* * * *

Noël had his share of problems with the fledgling medium, starting with *Together with Music*, which taught him some valuable lessons, such as insisting on adequate rehearsal time and taking personal control of camera movements. By the time he came to do *Blithe Spirit* the problems were no longer technical but personal and to do with his fellow players.

Everything appeared to start well. In December 1955 he notes in his *Diary:* "We had a successful reading of the play at the Bogarts' last Sunday and everyone read well. Betty Bacall will be good, I think, and anyhow she is word perfect, which is wonderful considering she was shooting a picture until yesterday."

The problem turned out to be Claudette Colbert:

I was right when I prophesied . . . that Claudette was likely to be tiresome. She has been e*xtremely* tiresome.

To begin with she arrived at the first rehearsal not yet knowing the words, after I had particularly asked her to be word perfect, with the first act anyway. She explained that this was not her method and that she had been a star for twenty-five years. In the second place, she is exceedingly bossy. In the third place, she can only be photographed on one side of her face, so all grouping of scenes has to be arranged accordingly. In the fourth place, she has changed her mind right and left over her dresses and now nothing is likely to be ready in time. In the fifth place, she is determined to play Ruth as a mixture of Mary Rose and Rebecca of Sunnybrook Farm, and very, very slowly. I have already had two stand-up fights with her, not very edifying and a hideous waste of time.

All this is a sad pity because, if she troubled to play the part for what it is worth, she would be very good. She is, within her limits, an excellent actress and these limits she imposes on herself. I have for years had a definite affection for her as a person, but these rehearsals are wilting it considerably. Betty is charming and no trouble; also, unfortunately, no comedienne, but she moves beauti-

fully, looks ravishing and is trying like mad. Mildred Natwick is wonderful; true, subtle and hilariously funny without ever being in the least grotesque. She will make a fabulous success.

Earlier Miss Colbert had been the recipient of a typical Coward facts-of-business-life missive. Having told her precisely what he was prepared to pay her—as opposed to what her agents were asking—he wags the proverbial finger:

I don't want to bring undue pressure to bear, but would like to point out that every dollar encircled by those pudgy French fingers will have to be extracted from these gnarled Scottish fingers. I do wish, Claudette dear, that you would look at the thing in a more Christian spirit; after all, Christmas is coming very shortly and I would like you to remember (a) The Manger, (b) that God is Love, there is no pain and (c) that you ate me out of house and home last Christmas . . .

I have painted you a picture for a Christmas present, so cast out of your mind all thought of that ermine stole; it is a very charming picture and if you don't like it, I shall be on hand with some seasonable suggestions as to what you can do with it.

Love, Love, Love, Love, Love—and let me know at once which way that fluffy little Gallic mind has decided to jump.

P.S. The next ugly scene, I suppose, is going to be about billing which is, and always has been, my *bête noire*. So I have arranged it alphabetically which will put the triumphant Betty Bacall before both of us! And if there's any argument, I shall appear *under* the title myself in tiny, luminous letters and leave you two glamour-pusses to straddle the farting title.

Mildred Natwick (Madame Arcati), Lauren Bacall (Elvira), and Claudette Colbert (Ruth) put on an off-screen smile. The actual filming was a less cheerful experience.

In mid-January he could look back in relative tranquility.

We went through the play twice during the day (Thursday) and gave a performance to most of Hollywood in the evening, not a very slick performance. Claudette uncertain and far, far too slow. After everyone had come backstage and said how gorgeous it all was and buggered off, I asked Claudette to play a bit faster, whereupon she flew at me and refused point blank. I kept my temper with difficulty and allowed myself only one riposte, which was when she said bitterly, "Don't worry dear, you'll never have to see me again after Saturday," to which I replied that it was not *after* Saturday that was worrying me but until and *during* Saturday.

The next morning I woke feeling dreadful. Someone had said that I was too "grim" in my scenes with Claudette, and I realized that if I or she allowed our personal feelings to show, the play would be ruined. So, crushing down my pride manfully, I called her up, apologized abjectly for everything including being born and coaxed her round to amiability. Then we went to the studio to see the kinescope of last night's performance. Oh, dear. It really wasn't very good. There were terrific arguments, in the course of which I roared for more close-ups and better lighting. Claudette and I remained Paolo and Francesca throughout the day.

Then we gave our second preview; not much better than the first, but a little. More people came round and said how absolutely wonderful we all were, and then Harry Ackerman (the director) informed me that we were two and a half minutes over time. So I sat down then and there and we cut judiciously some more good lines.

The next morning at 9:30 we saw the second kinescope. Owing to a genuine, but most unfortunate, oversight Claudette had not been told and had to be sent for. She arrived just at the end, fuming and with her hair in curlers. She insisted on seeing the whole thing through, so we left her to it, but not before I had delivered a calculated tirade to the "experts" about close-ups. I fairly let fly and when I had finished there was no comeback from anyone except the wretched Harry Ackerman, who said he had some other notes, to which I replied that no other notes were necessary and all I wanted was close-ups and more close-ups. Then down we went to rehearse and re-set most of the shots.

Meanwhile Claudette sat alone in the projection room facing the unpalatable truth that owing to her muddling and insistence on only being photographed from one side, during the breakfast scene particularly, all that was to be seen of her was her famous left jaw line, whereas I was in full face close-up throughout. We re-set a few shots but there wasn't, of course, much time.

We went on the air at 6:30, having worked up to 5:45. During this fascinating period I had about seventeen cups of black coffee, one hot-dog and a Dexamyl. When the play started I bounced on and, thank God, the curious miracle that happened to me last time happened again. I played without nerves and on nerves, and felt oddly detached as though I were watching myself from outside. The result was that the performance went like a bomb. Claudette played her hysterical scene well, her first scene too slowly and too sweetly, and managed to bitch up two of her best speeches by fluffing and gasping and panting. She wore tangerine lace in the first act, black and pearls in the second and a grey ghost dress that would have startled Gypsy Rose Lee. Her appearance throughout was charming and entirely inappropriate to the part and the play. We parted lovingly at the end and that was that.

God preserve me in future from female stars. I don't suppose He will, but I might conceivably do something about this myself. I really am too old to go through all these tired old hoops.

There was to be a postscript that Noël the dramatist could afford to appreciate in the euphoria of the notices. The next time he met David Lean, it was the less articulate director who had the last word. "Well, Noël," he said, "*you've* just fucked up the best thing you ever wrote."

*   *   *   *

"Noël Coward is a new and lively and welcome hand in TV's creative corral," wrote Jack O'Brian in the *New York Journal-American*. "He works like a longshoreman at his sprawling craft, which encompasses virtually anything in the spoken, written or acted English work." Another critic found the piece "light as thistledown and merry as an epigram tossed off in a glittering drawing room."

BRIEF ENCOUNTER

Brief Encounter was based on "Still Life," one of the nine one-act plays that made up *Tonight at 8:30*. Described as "A Play in Five Scenes," it was first performed at the Phoenix Theatre, London, on May 18, 1936.

PLAY SYNOPSIS
The refreshment room of Milford Junction station (probably based on Ashford, the local station for Goldenhurst). Behind the counter is the manageress, Myrtle Bagot, and her assistant, Beryl Waters. Sitting at one of the tables is Laura Jesson, a discreetly attractive woman in her thirties, on her way home from shopping.

At the counter there is a genteel flirtation going on between Myrtle and the ticket inspector, Albert Godby. A young doctor, Alec Harvey, enters and orders a cup of tea. Laura gathers her parcels together and goes out, only to return a moment later with a piece of coal dust in her eye from a passing train. Introducing himself as a doctor, Alec removes the grit. Laura thanks him and leaves to catch her train.

Three months later and Laura and Alec enter together. From their conversation, it is clear they have met several times since for lunch and visits to the cinema. We learn that Laura is married with three children and beginning to feel a little guilty about this new relationship, innocent as it is. Alec, too, is married with children. He tells her about his work. Although she understands little about it, Laura finds his enthusiasm attractive. They agree to meet again the following week.

Love among the teacups. The parallel "romance" between ticket inspector Albert Godby (Stanley Holloway) and Myrtle Bagot (Joyce Carey), manageress of the refreshment room, Milford Junction.

More time has passed. While the horseplay of the refreshment counter with its parallel courtship continues, Laura and Alec sit tensely, very different from their earlier lighthearted manner. Alec has suggested they go to a flat he has borrowed from a doctor friend. Laura finds the idea "cheap" and feels the time has come to call an end to a relationship that is affecting and upsetting them both. Both know that things have gone too far to turn back. Finally, Alec goes out, leaving her the address of the flat. Laura continues to sit there until her train is called. Then she picks up the paper and leaves herself.

Two months later and nearly closing time in the refreshment room, when a distraught Laura comes in alone. Only Beryl is on duty and waiting to leave. Alec enters, also upset and clearly relieved to see her. At first she doesn't want to talk to him. They had been at the borrowed flat when the owner unexpectedly returned and she was forced to run out, "feeling like a prostitute." She wants to end the affair and Alec, too, is well aware that time is running out for them. He tells her that he has been offered a job in Africa, which he now believes he must take for both their sakes. She, however, must decide. They once again admit their love and beg each other's forgiveness. Laura leaves to catch her last train.

Four months later and "Romeo and Juliet"—as the station staff have privately taken to calling them—are sitting at their usual table. It is to be their last meeting before Alec leaves to take up his new post. He tells her she will stay in his memory for the rest of his life. Laura miserably says she wants to die—to which he replies: "If you died, you'd forget me. I want to be remembered." With only a few last moments remaining they are interrupted by the arrival of one of Laura's acquaintances, Dolly Messiter, who proceeds to dominate the conversation, until Alec has to leave without being able to say the things he wanted to say. When he has gone, Laura suddenly gets up and goes out. A few moments later she returns, pale and shaken. She has just felt a little faint, she tells Dolly. Their train is announced and the two women leave together.

* * * *

As was so often the case in a Coward play, the stage directions and descriptions were integral to the drama. At a staged reading at New York's Lincoln Center the audience realised what it had previously missed by only hearing the dialogue.

The leading characters are described:

LAURA. She is an attractive woman in her thirties. Her clothes are not particularly smart but obviously chosen with taste. She looks exactly what she is, a pleasant, ordinary married woman, rather pale, for she is not very strong, and with a definite charm of personality which comes from natural kindliness, humour and reasonable conscience.

ALEC is about thirty-five. He wears a moustache, a mackintosh and a squash hat, and carries a small bag. His manner is decisive and unflurried.

The only surprise is Alec's moustache—presumably Noël's device for helping differentiate between the three different parts he'd be playing in any one evening. Looking at the production photographs, one can quite see why the moustache didn't survive into the play's various revivals.

The film version was made by Cineguild in 1945 and first shown in London at the New Gallery Cinema on November 26, 1945.

RW's cartoon captures suburban angst—not least Celia Johnson's "semi-deflated soufflé" of a hat.

CREDITS

In Charge of Production	Anthony Havelock-Allan/ Ronald Neame
Producer	Noël Coward
Director	David Lean
Screenplay	Noël Coward
Director of Photography	Robert Krasker
Art Director	L. P. Williams
Editor	Jack Harris
Sound Editor	Harry Miller
Sound Recordists	Stanley Lambourne/Desmond Dew
Production Manager	E. Holding
Assistant Director	George Pollock
Camera Operator	B. Francke

CAST

Laura Jesson	Celia Johnson
Alec Harvey	Trevor Howard
Albert Godby	Stanley Holloway
Myrtle Bagot	Joyce Carey
Fred Jesson	Cyril Raymond
Dolly Messiter*	Everley Gregg
Beryl Waters	Margaret Barton
Stanley	Dennis Harkin
Stephen Lynn	Valentine Dyall
Mary Norton	Marjorie Mars
Mrs. Rolandson	Nuna Davey
Woman Organist	Irene Handl
Bill	Edward Hodge
Johnnie	Sydney Bromley
Policeman	Wilfrid Babbage
Waitress	Avis Scutt
Margaret	Henrietta Vincent
Bobbie	Richard Thomas
Clergyman	George V. Sheldon

*Originally played by Joyce Barbour, who was replaced by Everley Gregg and the relevant scenes re-shot.

The synopsis provided to the critics summarises the way the film expanded the original play.

SYNOPSIS

Brief Encounter is the story of a chance meeting. The brief encounter which alters all our lives is an experience which most of us have had. To Laura Jesson, on her weekly shopping expedition to Milford Junction, the young doctor who takes a piece of coal dust from her eye in the prosaic L.M.S. refreshment-room is merely another traveller. This brief encounter of two people who weekly travel to

Milford Junction, the one to shop and break the monotony of the routine of domestic life, the other on his way to duty at the local hospital, is for them of great import.

Laura, contented, married, and fixed in her quiet domestic round, is disturbed to find that she is looking forward to seeing Dr. Alec Harvey again and when they meet by accident the next Thursday it is to make a definite appointment for the following week. Laura's weekly trip to Milford Junction is no longer to change her library books, visit the cinema and shop; it becomes the focal point of her life. She is essentially conventional. She loves her two children and is very fond of Fred, her husband, and the realisation that Alec means so much to her is an appalling one. Neither she nor Alec are strong enough to cease seeing each other, and eventually Alec—who is also married, but now deeply in love with Laura—persuades her to meet him in the borrowed flat of a friend of his, Stephen Lynn, whom he believes to be away. The unexpected return of the friend prevents anything worse than a humiliating flight for Laura and an unpleasant misunderstanding between Alex and Stephen Lynn.

This is a story in which the happenings are like life and not the conventional film script. Laura is hurt and unhappy, and it is with difficulty that Alex persuades her to see him the following week. He tells her that he has had a post offered to him in South Africa, which he will accept in order not to break up both their homes, but that he must see her once more to say goodbye.

When the final meeting takes place in the refreshment-room, where the

"She borrows her books from the Boot's library and eats at the Kardomah." Laura and Alec have their first accidental assignation. The waitress is played by Avis Scutt.

"I'll see you to your train . . ." The first realisation that something out of the ordinary is happening.

ticket-collector Albert Godby is enjoying an illicit stolen few minutes with the barmaid, Myrtle Bagot—just as he was when they first met—and against the background of ham sandwiches and buns—Laura and Alec know that they must part.

As they sit at a table waiting for his last train, their farewell is interrupted by the entry of a garrulous friend of Laura's, Dolly Messiter, a housewife on her way home to Laura's village, and—through the barrage of small-town gossip rattled off by her unperceptive friend—Laura and Alec hear his train come in, he says a brief word of parting, and she hears his train pull out of the station—and out of her life.

* * * *

Brief Encounter was to be the last collaboration between Noël and the trio from Cineguild, whom he now regarded as his "little darlings." So pleased was he with the outcome that he offered to let them film anything else of his that took their fancy. They, however, felt that they had now paid their apprentice dues and went on to exchange Coward for Dickens. Lean's next film was to be *Great Expectations* (1946). A year or so later Lean and Neame agreed to part company, since Neame was now anxious to direct himself.

All of them were lucky to be able to make the film in the first place. Back in the thirties Noël had cheerfully sold the rights to several of his properties to M-G-M—including *Tonight at 8:30*. While the rest remained under Hollywood lock and key—and still do—British producer Sydney Box managed to persuade the studio to sell him the rights to the nine plays. Over the

next few years he resold them piecemeal to J. Arthur Rank for a healthy profit. The first of them was "Still Life," which cost Cineguild £60,000, a lot of money for that time. The film came in at £270,000.

The choice of subject was almost accidental. Disappointed by the outcome of *Blithe Spirit*, the trio had started work on another project, which could hardly have been more of a contrast. It was *The Gay Galliard*, a costume piece about Mary Queen of Scots. Now this lady had crossed Noël's cinematic path before. Back in 1935 he had accepted his first starring role in a film called *The Scoundrel*, mainly because it gave him the opportunity to act opposite his "beloved Helen Hayes." In the event, Miss Hayes' prior commitment to a touring production of a play about "this rather boring historical person" prevented her from acting with him. This regal interference was not to be repeated.

To offer Cineguild an incentive to do one more Coward piece, Noël went away and reappeared ten days later with a first draft film script based on "Still Life." Although Lean was not happy with everything he saw there, once again he was hooked by the possibilities.

Were the comedy interpolations absolutely necessary? Havelock-Allan remembered Noël's firmness on the point: "(He) was an extremely skilful theatre writer and he knew that the story would have been intolerably sad otherwise. They provided some relief from the central situation, which was building up to be increasingly painful, both for the audience and for the two principals, for whom the audience feels deep sympathy."

Did Noël have to tell the events from A to B—just because that was the way he had written the original? Suppose we start the film with the scene where the couple part? Get the audience involved with them, asking questions about them? Then we tell the story in flashback. The rest was a virtual rerun of what happened on *In Which We Serve*.

Undoubtedly, the final film contains many such suggestions. As the professional filmmakers opened the story out from the original single set, they would often need linking passages that had been unnecessary in the stage version. Noël appears to have become a constructive collaborator. When the trio came up with a short early scene, Neame recalls, "He read it, remarked—'And which of my little darlings wrote this brilliant Coward dialogue?'—and used it just as it was. But on other occasions, when new material was needed, he would say—'Get out your little pencils.' We would get out our little pencils and he would walk up and down the room and out would pour dialogue—wonderful, brilliant dialogue. It came out just like that."

Circumstances sometimes dictated that their writing was done at long distance. Havelock-Allan: "At one stage . . . he was actually in India with an entertainment troupe; we managed to get cables through to him saying we needed thirty seconds of dialogue for the scene in the boat and we got a cable back giving us two lines of dialogue and saying: 'This runs forty-eight seconds; if you want to shorten it, take out the following words . . .'"

Once again the film editor's eye influenced the shape of the final film, even before the shots were locked into the detailed shooting script, which was invariably the Lean "Bible."

Then the *title*. "It's a little film," said Noël, "so it needs a brief something —something short." It was Gladys Calthrop, Noël's friend and personal artistic advisor, who came up with the final form of words.

* * * *

Brief Encounter is easily Noël's most successful screenplay; the film pulls together the promising elements in David Lean's emerging directorial style and turns them for the first time into a cohesive whole. The confidence the whole team had developed in each other by this time is clearly apparent.

Apart from *In Which We Serve*, an original screenplay, the other two collaborations had perhaps been overly faithful to the material with only the occasional embellishment. This time the story and characters—while faithfully rendered—are used confidently as the basis of something created with a totally different medium in mind. To use your source material without being used by it is arguably harder than starting from scratch. In the event, Noël manages to keep the narrative simplicity of the original, while extending its emotional complexity.

The "translation" begins with the film's point of view. Even though those who saw the original play grant that Noël "gave" it to Gertie, it nonetheless remained a two-hander, the story of two people sharing the same illicit emotion. But *Brief Encounter* is Laura's story almost entirely. Not only is she favoured in most of the shots but the story is linked by her interior monologue narration in which she "tells" her story to her husband, Fred, in her mind.

Noël made it a professional habit to know his characters before he wrote about them. His notes on "Still Life" contain her biography:

Laura Fayne—born 1900 in Cornwall—childhood school in Cornwall, holidays at home by the sea—married Frederick Jesson in 1922—solicitor's clerk in London. They live there for a few years then move to Ketchworth, Fred's home town. Fred becomes first of all Junior Partner in his father's office then, on the death of his father in 1930, Senior Partner at Jesson, Holford & Rhys. Laura's children, Freddie, aged 13, Betty, aged 11 and Robin, aged 9.

FACTS:
Laura's mother died of cancer 1918. Her father still alive and married again. One married sister, May and one unmarried brother, rather a waster, tea planting in Ceylon. [Note: Noël's late brother, Erik, had had the same occupation.]

INTERESTS:
Children, animals—books, average—mostly novels—Walpole, Phyllis Gibbs, Sheila Kaye-Smith, etc. Bored by Shaw—not particularly musical—loves movies, particularly gangster ones, "Silly Symphonies" (on account of the children) and "Travelogues."

He does the same for Alec:

Alec Harvey. Born Aberdeen 1901—educated Aberdeen High School—is in training Aberdeen university O.T.C. in 1918 aged 17. Decides to take up medi-

cine like his older brother, Gordon—is qualified—aged 23. Comes to London—attached to Guy's—rooms in Bloomsbury—meets Madeline Loring at a party in Hamstead—they marry 1925. In 1929 they settle in Churley where, through an agency, Alec has obtained a practice. They have two children. James, born in 1926 and John, born in 1928.

Alec's main interest outside his practice is "Preventive Medicine," particularly in reference to "PNEUMOCONIOSIS"

Anthacosis	-	inhalation of coal dust
Silicosis	-	inhalation of stone dust (gold Mines)
Chalicosis	-	inhalation of metal dust (steel Works)

Pneumoconiosis is a slow process of fibrosis of the lung due to the inhalation of particles of dust.

Alec's friend, Stephen Lynn, who was at the university with him is Physician to General Hospital at Milford and invites Alec once a week as assistant physician to take over for him, thereby giving him a chance for a certain amount of research of his special subject, as there are coal mines near Milford and lots of authentic cases.

* * * *

The Laura of "Still Life" is an outline; the Laura of *Brief Encounter* has the outline filled in. She is a real person of a certain class and time—the film is set in 1939—which is why so many other women could relate to her and turn her story into one of the perennial "women's pictures" of all time. Laura Jesson came within a touch of fulfilling the dreams of many a middle class, middle-aged woman who fantasises about the great love she would never know, except through the library books she religiously borrows each week. In Laura's case not from the public library but from the more upmarket Boot's, and not the vulgar "bodice rippers" but the more genteel fiction of Kate O'Brien, a writer who specialised in the conflict between romance and everyday life. In that sense, one of the morals of the film is that you are what you read.

Put this way, the film sounds like a psychological case study but it is much more than that, for Coward and Lean—and one must view the final execution as a true collaboration—are confident enough by now to temper emotion with irony. They let us smile before emotional tension causes us to laugh in self defence. One of the films Laura and Alec go to see on the Thursday afternoon outings is called *Flames of Passion*. It is so bad that they leave and go out for a boat trip, where the intimacy of this unscheduled event starts to trigger their latent feelings for each other. As things turn out, they would have been safer in the cinema.

The private joke here is that when Noël took an early play, *Easy Virtue*, up to Manchester in tryout, the local Watch Committee refused to licence it for performance under that name and he was forced to re-title it *A New Play in Three Acts* until he got to London. Meanwhile, he found himself staring at the poster for the cinema next door, where the current attraction was a film called—*Flames of Passion*! ("Perhaps the vigilance of the Watch Committee did not extend to mere celluloid," Noël wrote later.)

The whole structure of the film is Laura's subjective account of events and feelings and, time and again on repeat viewing, one finds oneself asking —is this what really *happened* or is this a visualisation of what she thinks she might have felt? Are we sometimes drifting into her novelisation of events? The fact that this objectivity is impossible on first viewing and irrelevant to one's involvement in the mood of the film is a mark of the technical skill with which Lean manipulates what we see and feel.

A good example of this directing of our attention comes in a particular pair of scenes which virtually open and close the film.

In the first the camera explores the geography and the denizens of the refreshment room, establishing the resident characters we shall come to know throughout the film; all of this is seen from an uncommitted point of view. Then at the back of the room we pick up this unexceptional middle aged couple sitting silent and sad. We overhear Myrtle, the manageress, repeating one of her endless genteel clichés—"Time and tide wait for no man, Mr. Godby"—which later takes on an added significance, should we happen to recall it. It is only when another character, Dolly Messiter, enters and recognizes Laura that we are allowed to move in and concentrate on Laura and Alec as the protagonists. Even so, we have been told nothing

"Poor, well-meaning Dolly Messiter . . ." Laura's garrulous neighbor (Everley Gregg) unwittingly interrupts the lovers' final moments together in the refreshment room where it all began.

about who the couple are or what their relationship is. Dolly proceeds to dominate the conversation of empty suburban chatter:

> *There is a sound of a bell on the platform and a loudspeaker voice announces the arrival of the Churley train.*
>
> LAURA: There's your train.
> ALEC: Yes, I know.
> DOLLY: Aren't you coming with us?
> ALEC: No, I go in the opposite direction. My practice is in Churley.
> DOLLY: Oh, I see.
> ALEC: I'm a general practitioner at the moment.
> LAURA: (*Dully*) Doctor Harvey is going out to Africa next week.
> DOLLY: Oh, how thrilling.
> *There is the sound of Alec's train approaching.*
> ALEC: I must go.
> LAURA: Yes, you must.
> ALEC: Goodbye.
> DOLLY: Goodbye.

> *He shakes hands with* LAURA, *looks at Laura swiftly once and gives her shoulder a little squeeze. The train is heard rumbling into the station. The camera pans with* ALEC *as he goes over to the door and out on to the platform.*

CLOSE UP OF LAURA

All of this we watch as uninvolved observers.

At the end of the film, when we have heard Laura's story—the scene is virtually repeated but this time the point of view is very different and imbued with what we know and what Lean would have us feel. The camera, as it were, is loaded. We now see things through Laura's emotional perspective.

For instance, we now discover the lovers in a much closer mid-shot. The decor of the room—which we know so well by now—is irrelevant. Now we have to hear what they are saying. Their grief at parting is not nearly expressed but, as Laura says desperately: "We've still got a few minutes." At which moment Dolly Messiter—whom we have not seen enter due to the tightness of the framing—literally pushes herself into the picture. The shock of the intrusion says everything about our involvement with the distracted pair. She is interrupting *us*. Every shot now focuses on Laura. The lighting changes, her thought voice and the Rachmaninoff on the soundtrack swell . . . Lean pulls out every trick to isolate her and focus on her.

David Lean considered that he was running a distinct risk by using the device of dimming the lights, so that the two main characters were the only things to be lit during the moments of most intense emotion. By doing so he hoped to increase the intimacy of the scene but he was afraid it might look tricky. In the event, he needn't have worried. Most audiences didn't even notice the effect, though they most certainly *felt* it.

Alec's train is announced and again, the hand on the shoulder. The gesture which had seemed so casual earlier now says everything about the pain of saying goodbye—without being able to actually say it. Behind the facade the defences crumble quietly.

In *Brief Encounter* David Lean learned to specialise in these dramatic juxtapositions. There is the early scene where Laura goes out on the platform to watch the express blast through and gets the speck of grit in her eye, which leads to the beginning of the brief encounter. Without becoming unduly Freudian, it is hard to avoid the interpretation that the unstoppable train symbolises the male excitement her life misses and which she sedately seeks in novels and films. At later dramatic points of the film the train is used as sexual punctuation, if one accepts this interpretation.

Again, near the end of the film—with Alec gone out of her life—we recall her words—"I want to die . . . if only I could *die*"—as she rushes out on the platform with the clear intention of throwing herself (like Anna Karenina) under the express. At that point the shot takes on a shocking meaning, emphasised by the camera angles Lean employs. Quite out of keeping with the ordered look of the rest of the film, the sequence starting in the refreshment room—uses disturbing tilted shots, more typical of the German neo-expressionist cinema, to reflect Laura's unbalanced state of mind. The rhythmic lights of the express flash across her face. And then normality returns and we re-enter the ordered world of Milford Junction.

"Miss Johnson's face and her walk and her eyes can tell a story or impart a mood . . . without the help of any narrative . . . Good acting needs no explanation."
—C. A. Lejeune

There are other, smaller touches that one only notices on a second viewing. To begin with their world is normal, even mundane, as they sit in tea shops, walk through shopping streets, laugh in the cinema. Later the night scenes take on a certain threat. As they run to catch Alec's train through the subway corridor linking the platforms, their shadows precede them, dwarfing them. Are they anticipating themselves with the shadows, threatening themselves by what they are doing?

Then, as Laura flies from the borrowed flat and the near discovery, we see her tiny, solitary figure from a bird's eye view, divorced from the safety of her cosy environment. As she passes a lamp post her own shadow suddenly elongates and looms at her. It makes an ironic counterpoint to Alec's earlier and equally ironic remark: "What exciting lives we lead . . ."

While it's hardly true to say that this kind of device abounds in the film, it occurs often enough to create an attitude towards the material and help us feel the powerful internal drama that is accentuated rather than diminished by the apparent ordinariness of the people and their situation. As Noël replied to a questioner almost a quarter of a century later: "I've always liked suggestion rather than flat statement. My best things are always written a bit obliquely. I wasn't at all sure it would work (with *Brief Encounter*) but it did." In another interview he would conclude: "The thing I like best about *Brief Encounter* is that the love scene is played *against* the words . . . He's a doctor and he talks about preventive medicine and the different diseases one gets, and all the time he's looking at her. And then she says, 'You suddenly look much younger'—which cuts right through and forces them back to ordinary dialogue." *Brief Encounter* has been called for good reason the quintessential "British picture," largely because of that quality of understatement.

Laura's words are those of a woman used to absorbing and accepting the words of others but never using them to express her own feelings, except on the most unexceptional subjects. Some things lie too deep for words with women like her. Noël's skill in writing for her is to let us know what is behind the ordinary words she does permit herself; how the retreat to domestic cliché signals her fear of the "awful feeling of danger."

The more obvious stroke of brilliance is in his choice of the film's music. When Laura and Fred are spending a typical evening at home—an evening that is proving extraordinarily tense for her—she turns on the radio. "Would some music throw you off your stride?" she asks, using one of the many phrases from the film that have entered the language of "camp." (To "shop until you drop" began life here.) The music she settles for is Rachmaninoff's second Piano Concerto with its soaring emotional flights. From that point it becomes thematic to her story, underscoring the highs and the lows, counterbalancing with its lushness the flatness of her words. Harold Pinter, a writer often compared with Coward, once described the process as "below the words spoken, is the thing known and unspoken."

The choice of the music was not unanimous to begin with. Musical director Muir Matheson believed every film should have a specially composed score and there were others who agreed with him. Many other British films of the period had "sold" on the strength of their overt theme music. Noël, however,

*Later the night scenes take on a certain threat . . . their shadows pre-
cede them, dwarfing them. Are they anticipating . . . threatening
themselves by what they are doing?*

was adamant. If he didn't actually say, "Extraordinary how potent popular classical music can be," he must certainly have thought it. What he actually said was, "No, no, no. She listens to Rachmaninoff on the radio, she borrows her books from the Boot's library and she eats at the Kardomah." End of debate.

* * * *

But what makes *Brief Encounter* a "woman's picture" is the woman herself—or rather, the way she is played. And for Noël, as for many thousands of others over the years, Celia Johnson has always been *the* Coward woman on film.

She first worked for him in *In Which We Serve* where, quite untypically, she asked him for the part. By way of auditioning her, she remembered later, "Noël began to spout bits of *The Walrus and the Carpenter* at me. What was the sun doing? Shining on the sea, I told him exuberantly, shining with all its might. If seven maids with seven mops swept it for half a year, he said, considering the situation gravely, do you suppose (and he dropped his voice because he wanted a very sad bit for the camera) that they could get it clear? I doubt it, I told him with an absolutely miserable face, and shed a bitter tear . . . We recited the poem at each other until we nearly burst, and it looked quite crazy in the rushes. But Noël seemed to like it and I got the part." (He also included the poem in the film for Johnson's character, Mrs. Kinross, to read to her children.)

She also got the part in *This Happy Breed* and then came *Brief Encounter*, where not even a hat that looked suspiciously like a semi-deflated soufflé could detract from that pointed little face and huge eyes. Gladys Calthrop, Noël's friend and his artistic advisor on the film, had felt the hat helped express the pre-war period and Laura's place in the even then dated class hierarchy—and one way or another it certainly achieved that.

The constant doubter, Johnson had to be persuaded once again that she could play the part. In one of her regular letters (October 1944) to her husband, Peter Fleming, away in the war, she describes how Noël came and read the part to her and her reaction to it:

> That is the trouble with being an actress. You do want to act even in such an unsatisfactory medium as films, and a good part sets one itching. And it *is* a good part. It's about a woman, married with two children, who meets by chance a man in a railway waiting-room and they fall in love. And it's All No Good . . . It will be pretty unadulterated Johnson and when I am not being sad or anguished or renouncing, I am narrating about it. So if they don't have my beautiful face to look at, they will always have my mellifluous voice to listen to. Lucky people.

The people on a Johnson set were also lucky, for—as well as being the Queen of the Crossword Puzzle—the lady was, somewhat surprisingly, an inveterate joker. A late example: "If the FBI guards the President and the Special Branch looks after the Queen, who guards de Gaulle? Le Gaulle Keeper."

The first choice to play Alec was Roger Livesey, an actor who had recently made a big success of *The Life and Death of Colonel Blimp* (1943). Livesey himself thought that he had the part, but then the Cineguild trio

Director David Lean (centre) discusses the next set up with Celia Johnson and Trevor Howard in the "Milford" street.

spotted an actor playing a small part in *The Way to the Stars* (1945) and Trevor Howard was signed for his first and best major screen role.

Looking at the final film, one sees a perfectly balanced couple and in describing it their two names often run into one another. In reality, Celia Johnson was by far the more experienced of the two and Howard's lack of experience was often a stumbling block for Lean. In the crucial scene when Alec describes what he does and the two of them recognise the real feelings rising behind the words, Johnson's instinctive ability captured the emotion at the first take. Howard experienced considerably more difficulty. To Lean's annoyance, as Howard gradually improved, Johnson's spontaneity gradually diminished.

There was to be another run-in between Lean and Howard, whom Lean found to be not a "very bright man." Howard simply could not understand the psychology of the scene in the borrowed flat. There were these two people, madly in love with each other, and now they had the opportunity to do something about it. Why did they just sit there *talking*?

Nothing Lean said could convey the mood. Finally, he simply instructed the actor to play the scene as written. Fortunately, Howard's insensitivity did not translate to the screen.

C. A. Lejeune was in no doubt that it was Celia Johnson who defined the film: "To my mind, Miss Johnson's face and her walk and her eyes can tell a story or impart a mood or reveal a confidence without the help of any narrative . . . Good acting needs no explanation." (Lejeune was one of the few critics to cavil at the narrative structure.)

The evocative poster used to advertise Brief Encounter.

Richard Winnington wrote in the *News Chronicle*: "Much of the power of the love passages is due to the acting of Celia Johnson, who, without manufactured glamour or conventional good looks, magnificently portrays the wife and mother meeting passion for the first time; who wants to die because of it and goes back to her husband and the books of Kate O'Brien, knowing that this golden brief encounter will die in her memory."

The *New York Times* critic felt that she gave "a consuming performance . . . she is naturally and honestly disturbing with her wistful voice and large, sad saucer-eyes."

Johnson herself was typically self-critical of her own performance:

I remember doing the scene with the train hurtling through and trying to get away from the chatting lady and thinking—this is the end for me, I shall finish myself off. And again, it had to be done in bits—one bit with the train, one bit with a close-up of just wind and things—and trying to keep it together is difficult, and then coming back into the station waiting-room. And when I see it now, I think, never do that again. That's quite wrong. But that probably happens to everybody doing films, one always thinks one could have done it better, one always thinks, "Never let me catch you doing that again," but you do.

In a later interview she came up with some sort of rationale of her undoubted appeal: "It's my *eyes*. It's a great advantage when everything is a blur beyond a certain point."

David Lean had his own explanation for her quality on film: "Movie acting is thinking, which a lot of people don't understand. If you're thinking right, it changes the way you walk, the way you put your head and it is all completely subconscious, because the thought just makes you walk or put your head or whatever it is in the correct way."

As an example he was fond of quoting the scene where Laura decides to join Alec at the flat and hurries to the station exit. "On her back you could read her thoughts . . . and all this thinking is transferred into the physical." When the scene had been shot, Lean congratulated Johnson and asked her how she had worked out what to do. "I didn't work it out," she replied, "She would just do that, wouldn't she?"

Of the film as a whole Lejeune concluded: "Noël Coward's *Brief Encounter* is, to my mind, not only the most mature work Mr. Coward has yet prepared for the cinema, but one of the most emotionally honest and deeply satisfying films that have ever been made in this country. It represents a confidence so utterly frank that few people will be simple enough to accept it as true."

In that last remark she was particularly perceptive. Early British audiences *were* made uncomfortable by the emotional power of the film and were inclined to make fun of the accents and habits of the characters in self defence. Until the film won the cachet of a prize at the Cannes Film Festival, the French saw no point in a love affair that never was but later adopted the film as if they had made it themselves. America strangely took to it from the first. *Time* called it "a heart-throbbing little valentine made with great skill."

Lean was cautious in his assessment: "As films go, it was inexpensive [but] it was not a big box office success. The greater proportion of filmgoers are under twenty-one mentally and physically; they go to the movies to escape from reality." A conviction which perhaps explains why his later career—when he could exercise full control over what he chose to do—was devoted to spectacular films that were anything but "inexpensive."

Noël himself was "delighted with it. Celia quite wonderful; Trevor Howard fine and obviously a new star. Whole thing beautifully played and directed—and, let's face it, most beautifully written." On another occasion, however—in his introduction to *Play Parade (Vol. IV)*—he clearly felt he was being disloyal to his first love, the theatre. "I am fond of both the play and the film with, as usual, a slight bias in favor of the former."

One review he particularly prized was from his old friend Mountbatten, who wrote from Government House in Delhi, where he was in the process of dismantling the British Empire:

> I have just seen "Brief Encounter" and cannot refrain from writing to tell you how deeply it moved me.
>
> I was proud to see it was made by the old "In Which We Serve" team, and there is no doubt in my mind that films of this sort must help to rebuild British prestige which is now temporarily eclipsed.
>
> Although I know that your personal inclination is to write for the legitimate stage, and this has of course a great value in keeping up home morale, I would like to suggest to you that the time has come when you should devote your remarkable gifts to a much larger extent to the cinema. Not only can you reach a much wider audience at home, but a good deal of good can be done in countries like India which show English speaking films in ever increasing quantities.

David Lean became the second British director to be nominated for Best Director in the 1946 Oscars. Celia Johnson was nominated for Best Actress. She lost to Olivia de Havilland in *To Each His Own*. However, *Blithe Spirit* did win the award for Best Special Effects.

From Lean's point of view, though, the most important accolade was perhaps Noël's when he first saw the film. "Well, my dear, I must tell you. You're the most resilient young man I have ever met."

Fifty years later the film is likely to found on almost every critic's top ten list. It takes time, it would appear, to accept the simple truths.

* * * *

There was to be an encore performance (of sorts) for Trevor Howard. On October 18, 1954, in a live NBC-TV programme called *Producer's Showcase* there were adaptations of "Red Peppers," "Shadow Play" and "Still Life" with Ginger Rogers in the Gertrude Lawrence roles, produced and directed by Otto Preminger. Breaking with the tradition of the original stage production, however, NBC gave Miss Rogers three different leading men—Gig Young as Simon Gayforth ("Shadow Play"), Martyn Green as George Pepper ("Red Peppers") and repeating his role of Alec Harvey ("Still Life"), Trevor Howard in his TV debut.

Seeing the production today, the most interesting aspect is the somewhat quirky casting of the smaller parts. Estelle Winwood as the overly mature actress, Mabel Grace ("Red Peppers"), Ilka Chase as Dolly Messiter ("Still Life") and "introducing Gloria Vanderbilt" as Sibyl Heston ("Shadow Play").

Variety was surprisingly kind: "Ginger Rogers had a personal triumph. No mean accomplishment as she changed moods and characters in three diverse roles." The *New York Times* was less so and found it "far from a happy choice of vehicle . . . an earnest eagerness to please but the subtlety, delicacy and perception of Mr. Coward's seemed largely to escape her grasp."

Considered objectively, what is surprising is that it wasn't worse. For a movie star of Ginger Rogers's magnitude to submit herself to the unblinking scrutiny of early TV lighting is remarkable; for the NBC powers-that-were to entrust Coward's literate dialogue to a producer-director, whose command of spoken English was never more than vestigial, beggars belief.

When Joan Collins produced her own TV version for BBC-TV in 1991 as part of the whole sequence of plays, she had the good sense to cast Jane Asher as Laura and John Alderton as Alec, reserving for herself the more showy part of Myrtle Bagot.

Nor was Ginger Rogers the least likely TV Laura. That accolade must be reserved for Dinah Shore, who essayed the part on her own show for Chevrolet opposite Ralph Bellamy as Alec on March 26, 1961. Several books on Coward will tell you that Noël himself appeared in this 1961 production. If only he had . . .

*   *   *   *

On December 11, 1974, a TV film version was made in the NBC-TV Hallmark Hall of Fame series and subsequently received limited UK cinema distribution.

CREDITS

Executive Producers	Carlo Ponti and Duane C. Bogie
Producer	Cecil Clarke
Director	Alan Bridges
Screenplay	John Bowen
Photography	Arthur Ibbetson
Editor	Peter Weatherley
Music	Cyril Ornandel

CAST

Anna Jesson	Sophia Loren
Alec Harvey	Richard Burton
Graham Jesson	Jack Hedley
Mrs. Gaines	Rosemary Leach
Stephen	John Le Mesurier
Dolly	Gwen Cherrell
Grace	Madeleine Hinde
Melanie Harvey	Ann Firbank
Porter	Christopher Benjamin
Alistair Jesson	Benjamin Ednay

A literary property that exists in one medium has come to be fair game for adaptation into another, as the movies have shown these past hundred years. There are as many adaptations of Dickens or Dostoevsky as there are filmmakers to make them and everyone is entitled to their "interpretation." The problem arises when someone tries to re-interpret someone else's *film*.

If Carlo Ponti and his team had given us a new "take" on "Still Life"—perhaps emphasising Alec's story rather than Laura's—that would have been one thing, but to tinker with *Brief Encounter*, a story re-conceived in purely cinematic terms, is perverse. To see this version is to appreciate the Coward/Lean version all over again.

The saddest thing on view is the way the makers clearly don't understand the thing they are copying and what makes it work in the first place. Gone is the linking narration which helps give the film its focus and emphasises that this is Laura's version of events. Gone is the "close-up" quality of the camerawork that lets you read events on the woman's face and excludes extraneous detail. Now we have a series of events—some of them the same as the original—mainly filmed in disinterested mid-shot, which occasionally happens to have the two principal characters involved.

The makers—for this is a collective crime—seek to open the film out, failing to appreciate that the claustrophobia was a key element. We see far too much of Fred (now Graham), busy being husbandly about the house or playing with the children. The original Fred was someone who existed slightly out of focus in Laura's peripheral vision. Only at the end did he move centre stage, when he welcomed her back. The balance of the relationship is ruined by making the husband "real." More here is distinctly less.

Laura, too, becomes less interesting by seeing her in her day to day life. Instead of spending her time in tea shops, libraries and cinemas, she now spends her one day a week in "useful" work at the Citizens' Advice Bureau and we are even obliged to follow one of her "cases." The point missed here is that it was because Laura's life is so circumscribed that she was open to the kind of feelings that were her undoing.

There are a host of other, smaller flaws, all of which emphasise the insensitivity to the subject. To replace the ultimate English woman, Celia Johnson, with the Italian sex symbol, Sophia Loren, is to create a conundrum within a paradox. Apart from having to explain her presence and introduce jokes about the pronunciation of *prosciutto*, for some reason Laura becomes Anna. Is Anna more Italian than Laura? (Petrarch didn't seem to have any trouble with the former.) The fact that Loren is Ponti's wife and may make the film more saleable in the United States is the real point of her casting.

Replacing the imaginary "Milford Junction" with the all too solid Winchester doesn't help either, because its importance to the story is misunderstood. The sense of *place* is totally missing, even though the place is real. In the original, the refreshment room and its inhabitants were fixed points of reference. Against its stolid predictability one could gauge the emotional temperature of the lovers. All of this is relegated to the wings. Instead screentime is taken to see Alec at home and Anna at work.

But perhaps the real clue is the *trains*. Gone is the age of steam and the thrill of "The Flying Scotsman" rushing through. Miss Loren has to contrive to get a speck of grit in her eye from a diesel and somehow that says it all.

We are living in a different world. Brief encounters belong to another time and we should leave them there in the safety of our memories.

* * * *

There was a footnote to the parting of the ways with Cineguild.

On June 21, 1947, "Ronnie Neame came to lunch and we discussed the possibility of filming *Peace in Our Time* [his new play based on the assumption that Germany had won the war and that England was now an occupied country]. Unfortunately he and David [Lean] won't work together as of yore, as they both must be directors. This is irritating for me, as together they were more efficient than singly."

In July del Giudice also wrote to Noël. Since leaving Lean and Company, he had started Two Cities but had now left that, too, and was in some financial difficulty. He had started his own production company, Pilgrim Films. He described it as "a pilgrimage of art. This land of yours, so hospitable to any man of good will, has given me the greatest chance any pilgrim could have."

He now wanted Noël to let him have the rights to film *Peace in Our Time*, which had opened earlier that month. "There will be plenty of offers for the film rights. There will be plenty of money offered to you but there will not be a more honest conviction of its various values . . . I think that this production, whoever is responsible for it, ought to be of great help not only to the British people for their understanding of the past and present sacrifices, but also to all the other people of the world. There is no comparison with any of the resistance movement films produced up to now. This is the most subtle construction of actions and reactions of what would have happened. And your mastery is shown especially where you deal with the psychological part of the average British character."

There the correspondence seems to end, perhaps because by this time Noël was tired of dealing with "Del" but at least in part because the play was not a commercial success, running for a disappointing 167 performances in the West End. While it was undeniably thought-provoking, it was too close to a recent reality for many people to want to have those particular thoughts provoked. The lucrative offers that del Giudice prophesied did not come to pass.

THE ASTONISHED HEART (1950)

"The Astonished Heart" was one of the nine one act plays in *Tonight at 8:30*. Described as "A Play in Six Scenes," it was first produced at the Phoenix Theatre, London, on January 9, 1936.

PLAY SYNOPSIS
The scene is the drawing room of the Fabers' London flat. Christian Faber is a famous psychiatrist. In the room his wife, Barbara, his secretary, Susan, and his assistant, Tim, are nervously awaiting the arrival of a woman called Leonora Vail, whom they clearly hate. The eminent surgeon, Sir Reginald French, enters and tells them "he" is asking for Leonora and there isn't much

Leonora Vail (Margaret Leighton) and Barbara Faber (Celia Johnson) were old school friends. Years later they meet by accident, share a pot of tea . . . and their lives are never the same.

time left. At which point the doorbell rings, causing Barbara to remember that it was at exactly this time a year ago that the whole thing began. As the butler announces Mrs. Vail, the light go down. When they rise . . . we see the same characters in precisely the same positions. A few changes of clothing signifies another time. The butler announces Mrs. Vail, an old school friend of Barbara's whom she has not seen since those days. They catch up on old times over a cocktail and Leonora pretends ignorance of what a psychiatrist does. Chris looks in to meet Leonora but his manner is offhand and when he has gone, Leonora jokes that she has given up her original plan to fall madly in love with him. As the two women part, Barbara accepts a dinner invitation for Chris and herself. Tim comes in looking for a Bible. Chris needs an appropriate quotation for a forthcoming lecture. They finally settle on "The Lord shall smite thee with madness, and blindness, and astonishment of the heart."

Two months later. Chris and Leonora in evening dress are in each others' arms. They discuss the affair they have embarked on. She confesses that she set out to make him fall in love with her, because he slighted her. He admits that his manner was a way of hiding the attraction he felt. How will Barbara feel? Chris knows she will be upset but will want whatever the two of them decide is best. Despite the way he feels for Leonora, he will always love his wife deeply.

Another three months pass and Barbara is waiting for Chris to return in the early hours. When he arrives, she insists on a talk about the situation. She tells him that his work is going to pieces. How can he help others when he is in such a state himself? Why doesn't he go away with Leonora for a while, as long as it takes for the affair to wear itself out?

Seven months later . . . It is midnight on the day before the first scene. Chris and Leonora are in the middle of a violent quarrel. She has had enough of his jealousy; it has killed her love for him. They both realise they have passed a point of no return. She goes to kiss him goodbye and when he has kissed her, he pushes her away so violently that she falls. He tells her that, because of his feeling for her, he has now lost everything that mattered to him. Even though the people who love him are trying to help him, he knows he is out of reach. She leaves. When he is alone, he walks to the window and throws himself out.

We now continue the first scene with the butler announcing Mrs. Vail. Barbara sends her into the inner room. A little while later she emerges. Yes, she tells Barbara and the others, it's all over. But she adds that Chris didn't recognise her. "He thought I was you. He said, 'Baba, I'm not submerged any more—and then he said 'Baba' again—and then—he died."

* * * *

The film version was produced by Gainsborough Pictures in 1949/50 and was first shown at the Odeon, Leicester Square, in March 1950.

CREDITS

Producer	Anthony Darnborough
Directors	Terence Fisher and Anthony Darnborough
Screenplay	Noël Coward
Photography	Jack Asher
Editor	V. Sagovsky
Artistic Supervisor for Mr. Coward	Gladys Calthrop
Music	Noël Coward

CAST

Christian Faber	Noël Coward
Barbara Faber	Celia Johnson
Leonora Vail	Margaret Leighton
Susan Birch	Joyce Carey
Tim Verney	Graham Payn
Alice Smith	Amy Veness
Philip Lucas	Ralph Michael
Ernest	Michael Hordern
Helen	Patricia Glyn
Sir Reginald	Alan Webb
Miss Harper	Everley Gregg
Soames	John Salew
Waiter	Gerald Anderson
Barman	John Warren

Mary Ellis made a short anonymous appearance as a patient of Faber's.

It was not the original intention to have Noël write the screenplay. Producer Sydney Box, who had originally acquired the rights to all the *Tonight at 8:30* plays and was in the process of selling them off to Rank piecemeal, invited playwright Warren Chetham-Strode (*The Guinea Pig*) to write one, presumably with the idea that this would give him a more complete "package" to sell.

Chetham-Strode reluctantly refused and—in a spirit of creative fraternity—explained his reasons in a 1948 letter to Noël: "It would need a good deal written in to bring it to a full length picture . . . Your work cannot be messed about." Noël, however, was clearly in favour of someone else adapting in this case and wrote urging the playwright to reconsider. This brought a fuller explanation. "It's not a matter of taking your play and adding twenty minutes . . . Whoever did the script of *Brief Encounter* [Noël himself] didn't only throw in a few extra trains . . . I feel that since the war we have come to hold more firmly to the values and security of work and friendship—rather than to the temporary enchantment and excitement of sex." There turned out to be a lot of good sense in the views he expressed.

* * * *

When the play did come to be filmed, there was a solid basis for the casting of the parts in the descriptions Noël had provided for the characters in the play text.

Christian was "about forty years old, tall and thin. He moves quickly and decisively, as though there was never quite enough time for all he had to do."

Barbara was "a tranquil, intelligent woman of about thirty-six or seven," while Leonora was "a lovely creature of about thirty, exquisitely dressed and with great charm of manner."

Of the supporting characters, Tim is "a nice looking man in his early thirties" and Susan "somewhere between thirty and forty . . . plainly and efficiently dressed as befits a secretary."

It did not take long to see Celia Johnson as Barbara and the elegantly neurotic Margaret Leighton as Leonora. Asked after the event to define the difference between the two actresses, Noël replied: "Margaret is so *chic*! Celia is so *understanding*!" He went on to elaborate, "The only thing that prevents Celia Johnson from becoming the greatest actress of her time is her monotonous habit of having babies."

Christian was not so obvious a choice.

Noël never intended to act in *The Astonished Heart*. The lead was originally to have been played by Michael Redgrave and shooting had actually begun in June 1949 when he notes in his *Diary:* "Drove to Pinewood . . . Saw rushes and rough cut. Margaret Leighton and Celia [Johnson] absolutely brilliant, but Mike definitely not right. Had a talk with him and then, on the way home, decided to play the picture myself. The situation now is tricky."

On the next day, however, he lunched with producer Anthony Darnborough, Sydney Box (then running Gainsborough Pictures—Michael Balcon's old stamping ground) and Redgrave. "It was mostly a duologue between Mike and me. Eventually he suggested that I play the picture myself. He behaved really and truly superbly, and I will always respect him for it."

The problems, however, were by no means over. The next day after that he went through make-up tests and rehearsed a scene with his friend, Graham Payn, who was playing Faber's assistant, Tim Verney. The studio backroom boys began to make their presence felt, which led to a confrontation—the first of many.

Spectacular scene in the afternoon when I had to send for Rank. [J. Arthur Rank was the leading figure in British films in the immediate post-war period and Gainsborough and Box were operating under his auspices.] His minions suggested that I play the picture for nothing as a gesture to the British Film Industry. Oi! Oi! It was a great and lovely drama in the course of which I beat him down and finished up with a virtual guarantee of £25,000 and a fairly large, as yet unspecified percentage of the profits. If the picture is a dead flop, I only get £5,000. If it is a moderate success and they break even and get their money back, I get another £20,000. If it is a smash success, I make on whatever is over after production costs.

Despite apparently endless hitches, Noël enjoyed the experience of filming again. His comfort level was raised by the fact that the first few days were devoted almost entirely to his scenes with Celia Johnson, by now the quintessential interpreter of his work. Her delicate appearance masked a tough professionalism that could compartmentalise work and personal life. Technicians who had worked with her on previous films would exchange stories of her fabled ability to concentrate on the take and then return to her inevitable crossword. In his biography of Noël his companion, Cole Lesley recalls one incident when Johnson's playing of a particular scene has brought tears to the eyes of everyone watching. Immediately she heard the word "Cut!," she walked off the set muttering—"Fourteen across is Rabbit."

Tim Verney (Graham Payn) has been asked by his boss, Christian Faber, to verify a biblical quotation. As secretary Susan Birch (Joyce Carey) looks on, Barbara finds it: "The Lord shall smite thee with madness, and blindness, and astonishment of the heart."

Despite the talent employed in putting it on the screen, something about the production refused to gel. In his *Diary* entry for November 10 Noël talks about working with conductor Muir Matheson on the score, which Coward had composed, after which he viewed the rough cut. "There is an essential lack in the picture . . ." he notes and attributes it to the fact that "I am never seen as being a great psychiatrist and the reasons for my suicide do not seem enough. It is nearly good but not quite."

In this he was being unduly self-critical. There are, in fact, several scenes in which Faber is seen with his patients and a very specific counterpoint in which he treats one patient, Philip Lucas, a successful writer, whose emotional problems turn out to be similar to Faber's own.

No, the problem with the film is fundamental to the original play—with the difference that what can be glossed over in a few minutes on stage is magnified in a full length film. How can a wronged wife (even one played by Celia Johnson) be so *understanding*? And how can an intelligent man like Faber unravel—or, as he would have it, "submerge"—so quickly and completely? David Lean might have found a filmic way to suggest the process visually, but in his absence what we are left with is melodrama that even its author can't handle.

The beginning of the affair convinces and the film version contains some of Noël's best understated ironic dialogue, as Chris and Leonora use words to test positions and wit as camouflage.

Barbara's mother is taken ill and she asks Chris to take her place on a theatre date with Leonora. The play disappoints and they go to the bar for a drink at the end of Act One.

CHRIS:	Would you like a drink?
LEONORA:	More than anything in the world. Can you tell what Act Two has in store for us?
CHRIS:	I've a fair idea.
LEONORA:	Strange! So have I. And the Third?
CHRIS:	I wouldn't be surprised if they fell into each other's arms.
LEONORA:	You must have second sight.
CHRIS:	No—just dismal anticipation.
LEONORA:	It would be quite shocking if we cut the rest of it, wouldn't it?
CHRIS:	(*gravely*) Quite shocking.
LEONORA:	On the other hand, I might get a complex about bad plays or something.
CHRIS:	My subconscious tells me we shan't be here.
LEONORA:	What a charming subconscious you must have.
CHRIS:	It's not always so obliging—but it has its uses. Shall we go?

It's when the raillery stops that the film's problems start and the web becomes hopelessly tangled.

Despite himself, Christian (Noël Coward) finds himself falling in love with Leonora—who is by no means averse to the idea.

Christian leaves Leonora for the last time and wanders the early morning London streets. He can see only one solution—and soon he will take it.

Sir Edward Marsh, a thirties socialite and patron of the arts, had offered Noël a comparable insight in a letter he wrote soon after seeing the original stage version. "It is evidently a fine and genuine piece of work, but for some reason it left me quite cold—and I now think the reason was the scene in which, after hurling Gertie to the ground, you sit down on the sofa and talk at her. This was 'unconvincing,' partly because it didn't seem likely she would put up with it, but much more because I can't believe that any man above the grade of coal-heaver or bargee, finding that he had hurled a woman to the ground, could be carried even by the most extreme stress of emotion into a denial of the elementary instinct (or perhaps it is the result of centuries of breeding) to pick her up again." And while the expression has a quaint ring to modern ears, the perception was instinctively accurate.

* * * *

From the single set of the original, the film is opened out. Characters are met at railway stations; we see Chris and Leonora's relationship develop at theatres and restaurants and in parks; Barbara and Leonora meet when they are both out shopping and take tea in an establishment that recalls *Brief Encounter*. All of these are conventional ways of setting film characters in context.

The directors would appear to have studied Lean's use of domestic locale. The flat in which the Fabers live and from which he operates his practice is explored by the camera, very much as the Gibbons's house was in *This Happy Breed*. There are frequent shots of characters—particularly Barbara, the deserted one—leaving rooms, while the camera stays behind as she retreats into the distance, emphasising her isolation. We are made very aware of the space that people are meant to share but which can also divide them.

On two separate occasions we are in Leonora's house. On the first we see the couple enter just before they admit their love for each other. The shot is taken from the landing looking through bannisters. Later, when the affair is over, we see the same shot. This time Chris stumbles out into the night and the bannisters look like prison bars.

The following sequence could easily have come from *Brief Encounter*. As Chris wanders through the streets, the camera peers down from a judgemental height, just as it did when Laura fled from her failed assignation with Alec. The shot seems to suggest that guilt diminishes the guilty.

The last sequence of the film encapsulates this use of physical space. Leonora, summoned to Chris's death bed, goes into a room and closes the double doors. Barbara—with Tim and Susan for company—makes forced conversation, while the doors occupy their attention. Finally, the doors open and Leonora emerges, tells Barbara of Chris's death and walks out of shot. Barbara walks up to the doors, pauses, then walks inside and closes them behind herself. Once again, the geography of the space defines character and relationship.

After the success of Rachmaninoff in *Brief Encounter*, the choice of music for the film was bound to be a key decision. Anthony Darnborough had a pianist on the set playing a selection from Chopin in an attempt to find something for Celia Johnson to play in one scene. At which point Noël emerged from the special suite he had been given, so that he could continue working on other projects during the interminable (to him) intervals between takes.

Diffidently (for him) he suggested that a tune from his new show might suit. Darnborough listened to Noël play it and promptly agreed. Knowing the next day was the director's birthday, Noël made him a present of the tune. A few days later he reappeared and announced: "I've written some stuff for you for the picture," before sitting down to play "a number of melodies and a main theme for the background music," all of which Muir Matheson subsequently orchestrated. Then, just as Darnborough was mentally totting up the cost of all this extra creativity, Noël added: "You'd better include it all in the birthday present."

* * * *

In the event, Noël's forebodings were realised. The New York critics were not kind. "Read the four morning notices . . . Very grudging. The afternoon ones were apparently worse . . . Oh dear. I really seem quite unable to please. If the picture turns out to be a flop, it will doubtless save me a lot of trouble. It's odd, but I really don't mind nearly so much as I should have done a few years ago. It would, of course, have been nice if they had all come out with blazing headlines saying it was the most marvellous film ever produced. It is only fairly good really, and censorship has certainly done nothing to improve it."

A cigarette break between scenes for producer Anthony Darnborough, Graham Payn, and Noël.

Celia Johnson seems more concerned with the daily "special" at the studio commissary than with the bons mots of her fellow diner.

C. A. Lejeune summed up the critics' reaction: "Seldom can expectation have wilted so quickly and so completely as it did in the face of *The Astonished Heart*. The film's worst fault is that it fails to touch the emotions at any point."

The *New York Times* concluded: "Mr. Coward is capable of doing better, though there are moments when the dialogue lets off caustic sparks. The writing and acting of the lead role by Mr. Coward himself are equally austere. His manner is too cool and reserved. *The Astonished Heart* is sluggish entertainment."

For the next forty years *The Astonished Heart* gathered critical dust and was scarcely shown. Later Noël was able to poke a little ironic fun at himself. In the short story "Star Quality" two of the characters go to the cinema, where they see "an exquisitely acted but rather tedious picture about a psychiatrist who committed suicide."

Towards the end of his life Noël referred to "Poor old *Astonished Heart*, I should love to see it again, just to find out if it really was as bad as they said it was." In fact, he never did see it again but he would have been pleased and amused to see it reemerge in the mid-1990s as a cult "art house" film.

*   *   *   *

In the years ahead there were to be many projects suggested, some half-started, others half-hearted. Mountbatten—still bitten by the film bug—was asking Noël in 1947 whether he had thought of doing "a musical film of your most popular and best known songs, which might be linked together by some sort of 'throw back' device such as you used in *In Which We Serve*?"

Throughout the early 1950s there were other desultory discussions. Alexander Korda—having wanted Noël for *The Third Man* (1949)—was particularly persistent. In September 1951 Noël records that Korda wanted to resurrect the Coward-Lean partnership "to do a movie about the convoys to Russia during the war"—a sort of *In Which We Serve* with icicles. ("Oh dear!")

A year later Korda had given up that idea and proposed a film of *Present Laughter*, to be filmed in 1953, presumably with Noël producing and starring. That, too, unfortunately faded to black.

This was by no means the first or last time this particular play would be seriously discussed.

In February 1946 Noël confides to his *Diary*, "Larry Olivier arrived with the disappointing news that he is not going to do the film." A year later producers Charles Miller and Lew Wasserman "want me to make a movie of *Present Laughter* for, obviously, any terms I want. I think they are shrewd boys."

Later—in 1955, when he is planning his three TV shows with CBS—he initially wanted to include the play with Claudette Colbert as Liz and went as far as to complete the adaptation. In the end CBS asked him to substitute *Blithe Spirit*. "Bill Paley (the head of the network) . . . is frightened of the sex angle . . . and fears angry letters rattling in the mail-box, written by outraged Methodists in Omaha complaining about illicit love being brought into their very homes by me and my sponsors, whoever they may be. This is irritating but I don't really mind because my object in the whole operation is to make money."

*   *   *   *

In February 1956 Noël

decided to utilize my peaceful mornings by writing a tentative film script. It is as light as the sensational omelette Coley and I made the night before last: a brittle, stylized, sophisticated, insignificant comedy with music and it is called *Later Than Spring*. It is about a fascinating *femme du monde* (Marlene) and an equally fascinating but prettier *homme du monde* (me), a fairly fascinating American young man and a young woman (possibly Van Johnson and Betsy Drake), and an articulate pair of companion secretaries (Graham and Marti Stevens). The intricate course of the story will be plainly obvious to the audience from the very beginning, and from the suspense point of view it will be as unexpected as *Cosi Fan Tutte*, but I hope the dialogue and lyrics and general treatment will redeem its apparent banality and make it a successful entertainment. At the moment I am enjoying it tremendously.

He went as far as to block out the cast—a habit he'd long used when contemplating a play. Presumably he found the characters lived for him, once he'd worked out their interrelationships. This list makes particularly interesting reading in the light of the ways several of the characters transferred virtually unchanged into either the unproduced musical play version or the later *Sail Away* (1961) and sometimes both. In other cases the names of characters are retained, though the characters are often significantly redefined.

It would seem likely that the parts Noël had in mind in his *Diary* entry would have been Prince Maximilien Valconi for himself and Tamarinda Bruce for Marlene; Skid Cabot (Van Johnson), Lollie Dukes (Betsy Drake), Nancy Foyle (Marti Stevens) and Monty Stein (Graham Payn).

Prince Maximilien Valconi	(An Adventurer)
Tamarinda Bruce	(A Film Star)
Verity Craig	(A Neurotic Divorcée)
Skid Cabot	(A Film Star)
Monty Stein	(Tamarinda's Agent)
Mrs. Spencer-Bollard	(A Professional Hostess)
Elmer Candijack	
Mamie Candijack	(A Family from Illinois)
Shirley Candijack	
Glenn Candijack	
Barnaby Slade	(A Film Director)
Lollie Dukes	(A Stenographer on Holiday)
Maybelle Fisher	(Ditto)
Irma Teitelbaum	(A Wealthy Lady)
Jonas Teitelbaum	(Her Husband)
Alvin Lennox	(A Writer)
Pipi Lafarge	(A Famous Dressmaker)
Nancy Foyle	(His Secretary)
Mrs. Van Mier	(A Bostonian Matron)
Elsworth Van Mier	(Her son, a Reclaimed Alcoholic)
Bonwit Franks	(A Decorator)
Tracy Waddinton	(His Friend)

Chief Steward Bothwell	(Principal Deck Steward)
Captain Lush	(Bluff Sea Captain)
Mrs. Warrilove	(Lonely Widow)
Doctor Mickleby	(Ship's Doctor)
Lawford Craig	(Verity's Husband)
Delia	(Tamarinda's Coloured Maid)
Amy Sprague	(Tamarinda's Companion)
Professor Aldemar Fingal	(Tamarinda's Psychiatrist)
Gregg Burton	(Tamarinda's Masseur)

A year later—Marlene having shown a teutonic lack of enthusiasm for the idea—he briefly reconsidered the project when he received a letter from Kay Thompson suggesting ". . . why don't you write a marvellous script for a marvellous movie for you and me?" (Thompson had scored her biggest film success earlier that year with Fred Astaire in Stanley Donen's *Funny Face*.)

The idea must have been appealing since Thompson was an old friend, but, in the event, the call of the theatre was louder and the film idea never progressed beyond the conceptual stage, though several of the minor characters' names eventually turned up—often in mutated form—in *Sail Away* (1961).

* * * *

In 1960 it was suggested that he might like to write the script for a film based on Churchill's *My Early Life*. ("The old boy himself is apparently very keen that I should, but I am not so sure.") By this time Noël's feelings towards Winston had somewhat soured and what would once have seemed like an honour was now more like a chore. There is no further reference to that project either. In the end it was Noël's friend and one-time *protégé* Richard Attenborough who made *Young Winston* (1972).

MEET ME TONIGHT (1952)

Three of the nine one act plays from *Tonight at 8:30* (1936)—"Red Peppers" ("An Interlude with Music"), "Fumed Oak" ("An Unpleasant Comedy in Two Scenes"), "Ways and Means" ("A Comedy in Three Scenes").

PLAY SYNOPSES

"RED PEPPERS"
The "Red Peppers" are a husband and wife music hall team—George and Lily Pepper—performing the same corny routines George's parents had used in their time. We find them on stage as they sing "Has Anybody Seen Our Ship?," the story of two sailors on a spree. As they make their zillionth exit, Lily drops her prop telescope.

We now find them in their dressing room in the middle of one of their many arguments. George blames Lily for ruining their number. She blames the conductor, Bert Bentley, for taking it too fast. While a non-musical act—the fading West End actress, Mabel Grace—is on, Bert drops in to ask them to time their exit faster. Lily takes exception to this and George, after initially siding with the conductor, takes his wife's part. The accusation of their being "a cheap little comedy act" is what does it. While anxious to observe the theatrical pecking order, he cannot accept criticism of his family "tradition." When Lily accuses Bert of being a drunk, he storms out.

Later, when the Red Peppers are dressing for their second number, the theatre manager, Mr. Edwards, arrives, obviously primed by Bert Bentley. He complains about the dropped telescope and goes on to say that the accusations against Bert are slanderous. Another row ensues. The Peppers complain the theatre is beneath them; Edwards says their act has always been a flop. The act is "called" and the room is cleared as they finish dressing.

On stage come the Red Peppers in white tie and tails to perform "A Couple of Men about Town." During the tap dance that ends the number Bert speeds up the orchestra. They try to keep up with it until George falls—at which Lily throws her hat at the conductor, crying "You great drunken fool!" The curtain hastily falls.

* * * *

"FUMED OAK"

In their suburban sitting room, furnished in fumed oak, are the Gow family—Henry, his wife, Doris, their snivelling daughter, Elsie, and Doris's formidable mother—predecessor of all the live-in matriarchs we are to see in later plays and films. Everyone bickers throughout breakfast except Henry—which only draws the fire of the others. Why was he late home the previous evening? Had he been drinking? He refuses to account for his movements beyond saying that he had been dining in town. The women resume their bickering without noticing he has left.

The evening of the same day. A skimpy cold supper has been left on the table for Henry, as the womenfolk are going to the cinema. When Henry enters, they sense something about him is different. Once again his mother-in-law accuses him of drinking, which Henry cheerfully admits to. He says he has something to celebrate. First, the anniversary he and Doris share. Not their wedding but the evening several weeks before that when she insisted she was "in the family way" and he must marry her—despite the fact that Elsie was not born until three years later. He then throws the supper all over the floor, locks the three women in the room and speaks his mind for the first time.

He explains that he has been saving up for years. He is now going to go off, see the world and start a new life. Doris is still young enough to earn her own living and Elsie can do the same. If she wants a father's advice, she will start by having her adenoids out. He says goodbye and walks out, slamming the door behind him.

* * * *

"WAYS AND MEANS"

Stella and Toby Cartwright are houseguests at Olive Lloyd-Ransome's villa on the French Riviera. Never rich at the best of times, they have now hit rock bottom, having lost heavily at the local casino the night before. Worse, they are well aware that they will soon be politely asked to move on. Sure enough, Olive soon breaks the news that other guests are due to arrive and their room will be needed. Soon after their train tickets arrive, making it obvious that their departure was previously planned. In desperation Stella sends her old nanny, now acting as her maid, to pawn the last of her jewellery.

In the equally early hours of the next day Stella and Toby are lamenting the loss of their last few francs at the tables. All that is left to them is to throw themselves on Olive's doubtful mercy the next morning.

Their sleep is interrupted by a burglar creeping into their room. Toby switches on the light and confronts the intruder, who has come to steal the jewels they have just pawned and lost. Having overpowered him, they discover he is Stevens, the chauffeur dismissed for philandering with his employer's wife. He knows and likes the Cartwrights and the feeling is mutual. Stevens is about to leave when Stella has a brainwave. Why shouldn't he steal the winnings of the new house guest, Mrs. Brandt? He can leave them bound and gagged to give them an alibi and share the takings with them. He takes little persuading and is soon back with the money and some jewels. They split the booty and Stevens politely leaves. Stella and Toby are laughing loudly as the curtain falls.

* * * *

The film version was made in 1952 for Rank and first shown at the Odeon, Leicester Square, in September 1952. In the United States it was retitled *Tonight at 8:30.*

CREDITS

Producer	Anthony Havelock-Allan
Director	Anthony Pélissier
Screenplay	Noël Coward

CASTS

"RED PEPPERS"

Lily Pepper	Kay Walsh
George Pepper	Ted Ray
Call-Boy (Alf)	Ian Wilson
Bert Bentley	Bill Fraser
Mr. Edwards	Frank Pettingell
Mabel Grace	Martita Hunt
Stage Manager	Toke Townley
Performing Dog Act	Frank's Fox Terriers
Chinese Jugglers	The Young China Troupe

"Fumed Oak"

Doris Gow	Betty Ann Davies
Mrs. Rockett	Mary Merrall
Elsie	Dorothy Gordon
Henry Gow	Stanley Holloway

"Ways and Means"

Stella Cartwright	Valerie Hobson
Tony Cartwright	Nigel Patrick
Lord Chapworth	Michael Trubshawe
Olive Lloyd-Ransome	Jessie Royce Landis
Princess Elena Krassiloff	Yvonne Ferneaux
Murdoch	Jack Warner
Nannie	Mary Jerrold
The Fence	Jacques Cey

* * * *

In the Coward canon *Meet Me Tonight* is something of a postscript—a plate of after-dinner mints, tasty but without substance. In the late 1940s and early 1950s Rank had been having some success with a series of anthology films—*Quartet* (1948), *Trio* (1950) and *Encore* (1951)—based on the short stories of Somerset Maugham. It was no wonder competing studios were looking around for other short form material and since, by this time, Noël had already adapted two of the one act plays from *Tonight at 8:30*—"Still Life" (*Brief Encounter*) and *The Astonished Heart*—there was no reason why a further three should not be attempted, particularly when there was no need to expand them to feature film length.

When he first discussed the project at the end of 1948 he had his ideal casting in mind. "Fumed Oak" would be played by Jack Warner and Kathleen Harrison—a nicely ironic piece of casting, since they were known for their portrayal of the popular film couple, the Huggetts, almost Cowardesque in their cheerful Cockney working class manner.

"Red Peppers" would be Jack Hulbert and Cicely Courtneidge, a beloved real life husband and wife team of the period whose own stage history—while significantly more successful—had put them on the bill with many an act like the one they would be portraying.

His third choice at that time was for the Victorian parody "Family Album," and for that he had Margaret Leighton and Graham Payn in mind.

In the event, things turned out rather differently. The only one of the original actors to actually appear was Jack Warner and only in a supporting role. By way of compensation, however, there were one or two members of the Coward film "repertory company"—Kay Walsh (*In Which We Serve, This Happy Breed*) as Lily Pepper and Stanley Holloway (*This Happy Breed, Brief Encounter*) as Henry Gow.

Of the three "Red Peppers" gives the most pleasure, since it provides images to one's mental replay of the audio recording Noël and Gertie made of the piece. At times Kay Walsh even manages to look a little like Gertie and has the same kind of attack. The trouble is with Ted Ray as George Pepper. At the time Ray was a popular radio comedian in the American style of staccato wisecracks. He had little range and was not particularly "loveable" in his professional persona; consequently, he evoked little sympathy for the character he played. Seeing Olivier years later as Archie Rice (*The Entertainer*), another failed comedian, made one realise that it probably takes an actor to "comment" on what it is to be a funny man. Undoubtedly Noël's own original performance revealed that too. The real life professional comic is too concerned with the mechanics of his craft. There is *still* a film to be teased out of "Red Peppers."

Anyone who does so will do well to take heed of Noël's own assessment, which he applied to the whole *Tonight at 8:30* canon: "The point of 'Red Peppers' was to spend an evening seeing Noël Coward and Gertie Lawrence *not* playing Noël Coward and Gertie Lawrence, that is the fun. The moment you do one of these little plays for real, they don't exist." In so saying, he was perhaps casting a rueful backward glance at his own effort to do just that with *The Astonished Heart* a couple of years earlier.

"Fumed Oak" is a misogynistic monologue nicely handled by Stanley Holloway as the filler in the sandwich, but "Ways and Means" refuses to leave the page and the stage for the screen. The question must be why Noël let himself be talked into using it instead of "Family Album" when he himself said of the piece that it was "a 'twentyish' little farce set in the then fashionable South of France. I never cared for it much . . ."

He even had to tip his hat to the censors by changing the ending. Instead of receiving their ill-gotten gains, the Cartwrights are double-crossed by the thief, who then falls into the hands of the gendarmes.

He cared for it even less when he saw the completed film. "Absolutely awful—vilely directed and, with one or two minor exceptions, abominably acted. Came home and rested."

The *New York Times* was not quite so damning and found it "a varied entertainment short on excitement but funny and trenchant enough for many tastes."

Perhaps the most depressing part was to read the credits and see the name of Anthony Havelock-Allan. David Lean and Ronald Neame had long since gone their separate ways and Cineguild dissolved. Havelock-Allan was now an independent producer. The project was, he admitted later, "just to have something to do, more or less" and he was inclined to blame Pélissier (actress Fay Compton's son): "He had many different talents but none of them big enough to make a real impact." While the verdict may have been supported by *Meet Me Tonight*, it was a little unfair to the director's overall output, which included box office successes such as *The History of Mr. Polly* (1949) and *The Rocking Horse Winner* (1949).

* * * *

"Red Peppers" also became something of a TV standby. As early as 1951 NBC-TV put on a production with Rex Harrison and Beatrice Lillie as George and Lily Pepper. In 1954 Ginger Rogers played opposite Martyn Green also for NBC-TV while in 1960 the parts were taken by Art Carney and Elaine Stritch. In the United Kingdom Bruce Forsyth and Dora Bryan starred in a 1969 BBC production with the considerable support of Anthony Quayle, Cyril Cusack and Edith Evans as Mabel Grace.

PRETTY POLLY (1967)

Adapted from a short story, "Pretty Polly Barlow." In the United States the film was called *A Matter of Innocence*.

STORY

Polly—a frumpish, ugly duckling of a girl—accompanies her rich, cantankerous aunt on a holiday to Singapore, where she is bullied and ordered about from pillar to post. Before long, however, the offending relative dies after taking a swim too soon after a heavy lunch and Polly is free to indulge herself in the expected transformation from duckling to swan. With the encouragement of an Indian, who acts as her guide and advisor, she discovers the joys of make-up and fashionable clothes. Soon the swan turns into a siren.

CREDITS

Universal	
Producers	Marshal Backlar/Noel Black
Director	Guy Green
Screenplay	Keith Waterhouse and Willis Hall
Photography	Arthur Ibbetson
Editor	Frank Clarke
Music	Michel Legrand

CAST

Polly	Hayley Mills
Mrs. Innes-Hook	Brenda de Banzie
Robert Hook	Trevor Howard
Amaz	Sashi Kapoor
Preston	Dick Patterson
Lorelei	Kalen Lui
Miss Gudgeon	Patricia Routledge
Critch	Peter Bayliss
Mrs. Barlow	Dorothy Allison
Ambrose	David Prosser

There was talk in the early stages of planning that Noël would not only write a theme song for the film but also play a cameo role. In the end he did neither.

If an interminable series of contractual problems didn't warn Noël that the project was jinxed, the outcome certainly did. In his *Diary* (July 1967) he notes: "I watched, with mounting irritation, the film of *Pretty Polly* which, as I deduced from the first script, was common, unsubtle and vulgar. Nobody was good in it and Trevor Howard was horrid. When I think of his charm and subtlety in *Brief Encounter*. Hayley, poor child, did her best, but there was no hope with that script and that director. Guy Green should have remained a cameraman."

Later Waterhouse claimed morosely that he and Hall had warned Noël that the piece lacked a third act. To which Noël replied firmly, "It's a two act story."

Wilfred Sheed summed up critical opinion: "It came and went this winter, leaving a slight trace of camphor and old knitting needles." The *New York Times* was slightly kinder: "It is entertaining in a way very bad movies are."

PART THREE

Noël Coward: Film Actor

I have had rave notices and several
headlines saying I "steal" the picture . . .
This, of course, is true but it is petty
larceny.

—NOËL COWARD

* * * *

Playing with Noël is a lot like playing with God.

—MICHAEL CAINE

* * * *

I don't think I want to play a very, very long movie, but
I do like nipping in and playing a good scene or two. I
am much more relaxed in front of the camera than I used
to be.   —*Diaries (October 1962)*

In the light of his many and early successes, it's a remarkable thought that until
In Which We Serve (1942) Noël had only appeared in two acting roles in films.

The first was in D. W. Griffith's "soul-stirring spectacle," *Hearts of the
World*, made in England in 1917. It was the first time Griffith had filmed in
England and it was prompted by an offer from the British Government,
which badly wanted a propaganda film to influence American opinion toward
the Allied cause. The film was finally co-financed by them, and Adolph
Zukor and Griffith (using two pseudonyms) wrote the screenplay.

The film was not destined to be remembered as one of Griffith's major
achievements. It was one more variant on his standard theme of a woman's
maturity. Gish begins as an innocent girl, surrounded by farm animals, with
no greater ambition than that the Boy will always love her. By the end of the
film she is a woman who is able to kill one of the advancing Germans when
the need arises. She is first seen playing with ducks but the woman we leave
is one who knows about life's miseries and suffering—as well as its moments
of happiness. It has all the hallmarks of being a routine vehicle for the Gish
sisters, who were contracted to Griffith at the time, but the subject matter
seemed to hold little interest for the director on this occasion. "Viewed as
drama," he was quoted as saying, "the war is in some ways disappointing."

So was the film—from a propaganda point of view. By the time it
was shown, the United States was in the war anyway. However, there were
consolations. *Hearts* made a profit and the battle footage—shot in England
and California—was later reused in *The Girl Who Stayed at Home* (1919).

*Opposite: Noël wonders if Lilian Gish has noticed he has started
pushing his barrow towards the camera instead of away from it.*

The teenage Coward was an extra, "paid, I think, a pound a day, for which I wheeled a wheelbarrow up and down a village street in Worcestershire with Lillian Gish."

In her autobiography, *The Movies, Mr. Griffith and Me*, Gish recalls "a darling seventeen year-old English boy, whom Mother promptly added to her brood. He had an original mind and a sense of theatre. In one scene the French girl I was playing packed her possessions and left home . . . This young actor was supposed to help me by pushing the loaded wheelbarrow down the street. At his own suggestion the boy pushed the wheelbarrow toward the camera instead of away from it. The boy was Noël Coward and the film was his first."

The memory stayed with Gish. As late as 1964 she is writing to Noël: "There am I, waving, as you chart your course on the small river in 1917 to float down to the great seas of the world, while I remain moored to the little raft!!! . . . You are certainly God's favourite child."

This led to one of the first and most important lessons he ever received in film acting. Noël recalled the experience to an audience at the National Film Theatre over fifty years later. "He [Griffith] was most awfully considerate to this raw beginner . . . At one point he said—'I shouldn't do *that*, if I were you.' I said—'What am I doing?' 'Acting.' I said—'Well, I'm not playing myself. I have to do a bit of that.' He said—'Have you by any chance noticed where the camera is?' I said—'Oh, dear me, no,' because I was too busy *at* it. He said—'It's *here* and so your underlip is a foot wide. And so, if I were you, I shouldn't pitch to the back of the gallery.'" He was to receive precisely the same choice some thirty years later from Carol Reed, while shooting *Our Man in Havana*. "I was still playing to the back of the gallery."

* * * *

He was to make oblique reference to his film experience in *I'll Leave It to You* (1919), when a character, Sylvia, becomes a movie actress and recalls "that day in the middle of the village street, when I had to do three 'close-ups' on top of one another." To which her mother observes, "Sounds vaguely immoral to me."

HEARTS OF THE WORLD (1917)

CREDITS

Director	D. W. Griffith
Screenplay	M. Gaston de Tolignac
	(Translated by Capt. Victor Marier)

CAST

Lilian Gish	Robert Harran
Dorothy Gish	Kate Bruce

STORY

Set in a 1912 French village during the buildup to World War I, the story is of an American artist who falls in love with a local girl, only to have the war intervene.

Fade out. Fade in to 1935. By this time Noël Coward is a name to be reckoned with on both sides of the Atlantic as dramatist, actor, composer, lyricist and all round celebrity. *Hay Fever, Fallen Angels, Private Lives* and *Design for Living* are already behind him—the last two even committed to film. The experience of watching his work transferred to the new medium had, by and large, not been a rewarding one, but when he was invited to star in a film, he had little hesitation in accepting. The *New York World Telegram* announced: "Noël Coward Kliegs As A Bathing Beauty In His Maiden Mugging."

The film was *Miracle on 49th Street*, which became *The Scoundrel*. It was to be made by Paramount, a major studio, not in Hollywood but in the Astoria Studios in Brooklyn, New York, and Noël was guaranteed it would be finished in thirty days, so that he could resume his world travels. "What really induced me to try films," he told an interviewer, "was that I wanted the experience."

He wrote to his mother:

My picture is going to be very good, I think. The story and dialogue is marvellous but, oh dear, I'm afraid it will upset you, as it is very tragic and I have to die in it! I play half of it as a dead man! I will send you a complete script soon so you can read it and be fully prepared.

I have done some good tests and they all seem to think that I am fine—so that's that! I get up at seven a.m. and don't get back until the evening, when I go straight to bed. It's a hard routine but actually I rather enjoy it!

He went on to express his admiration for the talents of Ben Hecht and Charles MacArthur, the well-known playwrights who were writing and directing the film—a slightly unexpected eulogy in the light of Hecht's earlier claim that in adapting *Design for Living* a couple of years before he had kept only one line of the original play. Having seen their previous independent film (*Crime without Passion*): "For the first time I realised a film could be produced by a few persons . . . Here is a greater chance of producing something worthwhile." Later Noël amplified his reasons: "I agreed to do it because I thought the idea was good and, most particularly, because I was promised that Helen Hayes, whom I love and admire, would play the young poetess. [Hayes was then married to MacArthur.] However, at the last minute she was unable to get out of some contract [touring in *Mary of Scotland*] and the part had to be re-cast. Finally, after much trial and error, Julie Haydon walked into the office, read the part sensitively and was engaged. The picture was made quickly and fairly efficiently; most of its speed and efficiency being due to Lee Garmes, the cameraman." Garmes had already made his reputation by creating a distinctive look for Dietrich in von Sternberg films such as *Morocco, Shanghai Express* and *Dishonored*.

Noël found the direction of Hecht and MacArthur less admirable. It was, he recalled, "erratic, and I, who had never made a picture before, was confused and irritated from the beginning to the end." What particularly annoyed him was what he, even as an amateur in the game, considered their lack of professionalism. They spent no time briefing the actors, played backgammon all day and only tore themselves away from the board when an actual take was called. Noël was allowed to do whatever he wanted and to change the material at will. He also insisted on seeing all the rushes, a habit which provoked a fellow actor, *New Yorker* writer Alexander Woollcott, to call him the "Czar of all the rushes."

On one occasion he exercised this freedom in dramatic fashion. Julie Haydon was not a particularly skilled player herself and her obsession with her coiffure at all times began to get on Noël's nerves. When the script arrived at a big emotional scene, Noël took advantage of directorial laxness to brief the camera crew personally to continue shooting no matter what. Then, when the scene began, he started to tousle the lady's hair-do violently. She reacted emotionally and the result was considered the highpoint of her performance.

One of the few small pleasures of the film was its New York location. Noël was able to persuade various of his friends to visit the set and play (unpaid and uncredited) walk-on parts. The Lunts, critic George Jean Nathan (who fell in love with and later married Haydon), novelist Edna Ferber, Katharine Cornell, Ina Claire, Elisabeth Bergner and agent Leland Hayward may be spotted by the eagle of eye. (In the same spirit Noël was to take part in a crowd scene in Katharine Hepburn's film *The Philadelphia Story* when he happened to be staying with her costar, his friend Cary Grant.) By way of partial compensation, daily at noon three taxis would arrive at the studio, complete with waiters and lunch from "21."

In March—en route for Honolulu after a stopover in Hollywood—he writes to his mother:

> Well, dear, I'm afraid I shall have to fall for the movies after all. I've almost but not quite decided to do three pictures in two years for Metro-Goldwyn-Mayer. It only means six weeks to two months at a time and they're offering me such marvellous terms it seems a little silly to refuse. I asked for a percentage of the gross, which they never give, and to my amazement they said yes! So I quickly got on to a boat (the *S.S. Malolo*) and disappeared. I don't intend to sign any contracts until after the Hecht-MacArthur picture has opened . . . I have a dreamy artistic feeling that I shall get a higher percentage still after that! All this is strictly secret at the moment, so don't tell a soul.

The Scoundrel, Noël later wrote, "was hailed with critical acclaim. I made a success in it and so did everyone concerned, but I still wish that it and they and I had been better." In fact, the film was only a success in the big cities—middle America saw little in it to empathise with—and later with art house audiences around the world. "A critic's picture with limited box office appeal," *Variety* concluded. Over the years it has grown to the status of a cult movie. Noël was not paid much for appearing in it ($5,000), but he did receive a share of the profits—or so he thought. Then it appeared that he had signed them away as an investment in Hecht and MacArthur's next picture, *Down To Their Last Yacht*, which flopped. It should have taught him to read the small print in his contracts but, unfortunately, it didn't.

The film had one immediate and enthusiastic fan—Marlene Dietrich. She phoned Noël straight after seeing it but he refused to take the call, assuming it to be a hoax. Only after persevering did she get through with her congratulations on his performance. The line remained open for the rest of their lives.

One critic described the film as "Barbs of dated wit despatched by a splendid cast. Nonsense, but great nonsense." Another called it "a minor masterpiece of literary caprice," while Henry Clark saw it as "a new and rare kind of picture that combines art with fantasy, along with techniques in acting, directing and photography that were well ahead of the times." William Whitebait (*New Statesman*) found it "an unmistakable whiff from the gossip column world which tries hard to split the difference between an epigram and a wisecrack." The *New York Times* felt that it contained "the most dazzling writing this column has ever heard on the screen . . . it is a distinctly exhilarating event . . . regardless of whether you look upon it as art or spinach."

Noël's own performance was generally praised. "Coward's British ability at underplaying on stage turns out to be eminently well suited for the more intimate scale of the screen close up," said the *New York Herald Tribune*, while the *Sun* found his "gaunt, deliberating, cynical publisher unwilling to let himself feel deep emotion, as the drowned man strangely sent back for his one chance at peace, he has an uncanny quality. It is not a performance easily forgotten." Noël himself observed: "I thought I was very good in the parts when I was dead." Critic André Sennwald was also taken with Noël's performance ("You have to hear him reciting a line like 'It reeks with morality' —stressing the r's to make it exquisitely funny—to know how good he can be") and named the film one of the year's ten best, but another reviewer came

Egocentric publisher Tony Mallaré (Noël Coward) casually seduces the naïve young Cora Moore (Julie Haydon), only to make an implacable enemy of her previous admirer, Paul (Stanley Ridges).

Cora is now deeply in love with Mallaré but emotional depth is a concept totally alien to him. Any passing physical resemblance to Noël Coward is presumbably intentional.

Killed in an air crash, Mallaré is allowed a brief return to earth. He may save his soul if within one month he can find one person who truly loved him and mourns his death.

to the opposite conclusion: "It starts out Oscar Wilde and ends up Eugene O'Neill screwy, with Noël Coward talking to himself over his shoulder." The film received no Oscar nominations. The American Legion of Decency gave the film its ultimate intellectual accolade by condemning it.

THE SCOUNDREL (1935)

CREDITS
Paramount Pictures

Producers, Directors and Writers	Ben Hecht and Charles MacArthur
Photography/Assistant Director	Lee Garmes
Editor	Arthur Ellis

CAST

Tony Mallaré	Noël Coward
Cora Moore	Julie Haydon
Paul Decker	Stanley Ridges
Julia Vivian	Martha Sleeper
Maurice Stern	Eduardo Ciannelli
Jimmy Clay	Ernest Cossart
Rotherstein	Lionel Stander
Carlotta	Rosita Moreno
Maggie	Hope Williams
Mildred Longville	Everley Gregg
Mrs. Rollinson	Helen Strickland
Slezack	Harry Davenport
Luigi	William Ricciardi
Scrubwoman	Isabelle Foster
Fortune Teller	Madame Shushkina
And Alexander Woollcott	

The film opened on May 1, 1935, and cost $190,000.

STORY
Tony Mallaré, a young publisher, gets pleasure from using other people for his own ends. Drowned in an aeroplane crash, he is condemned to return to the world for one month in an effort to find someone who will mourn his death.

* * * *

It would be twenty-one years before Noël appeared before the camera in someone else's film and then he was in the best of company. When impresario Mike Todd decided to make a movie—or anything else, for that matter—he didn't take no for an answer. In the early 1950s he took it into his head to film Jules Verne's famous adventure story, *Around the World in Eighty Days*.

David Niven would play the part of Phileas Fogg, the Victorian clubman who accepts a wager that he cannot circumnavigate the globe in less than eighty days; Cantinflas, the Mexican comedian, would play the part of his faithful servant, Passepartout. To set the film apart from other spectacles that were being made to stave off the competition of television, Todd had the idea of casting actors and actresses who would normally command star status in cameo roles. He invited Noël to be one of them.

In his *Diary* for July 1955 Noël records: "I have agreed to do one small scene (two days' work) . . . For this I will not be billed or paid but he will give me a nice Corot or Bonnard or Vuillard, to be chosen when I get back."

As he said later: "One of the reasons I accepted the part was that, having seen *Oklahoma!* I thought that if Todd-AO could make acres of green corn look so lovely, it could do the same for me. Todd was trying to get a herd of buffalo for the film. It was easier to get me . . . I was fascinated to see that the script described my role as 'superior and ineffably smug.' It was clearly type-casting."

A month later he sounded less cheerful. "There has been a great fuss and fume because Mike Todd asked me to ask Larry (Olivier) to play the scene with me." The proposed scene was between Roland Hesketh-Baggott (Noël), who owns an employment agency for butlers, and Foster, Fogg's retiring servant.

> Larry, as usual, wavered and said he might, then finally said he wouldn't. Today Mike called me to say that Johnny Gielgud was going to do it.
>
> *Friday, September 2.* On Tuesday I got up at crack of dawn and went to Elstree. It was a very successful day and Johnny and I managed to do the whole scene. Johnny was charming to work with. He was, as usual, a little false in his performance but very effective. If Larry had played it in a dreadful, refined Cockney accent, it would have been hilarious; as it was, it was perfectly all right. All the people at the studio were extremely nice and I thoroughly enjoyed the day. Before leaving, Mike presented me with a cheque for £100 which, together with the Bonnard, brought my day's salary up to £4,600. Mustn't grumble.

There has always been a strong suspicion that Noël wrote—or perhaps *re*-wrote—the scene in which he and Gielgud appeared, and certainly his archives contain such a scene which is separately typed and not extracted from a master script. If it were not a Coward original, it is hard to explain why he would have kept it in this form when he kept none of the other film scripts in which he appeared.

Originally the character he played was called "Smythe-Baggott." By the time of filming that had been changed to "Hesketh-Baggott."

*   *   *   *

In October Noël attended the film's premiere, which he considered "a great big smash hit. It really is a fascinating picture and none of the multitude of star bit-players attempts any hogging."

Not all the critics concurred. David Robinson decided that "Michael Todd's 'show,' shorn of the ballyhoo and to critics not mollified by parties

An emollient Hesketh-Baggott (Noël) and an apprehensive Foster (John Gielgud).

In Michael Anderson's Around the World in Eighty Days *(1956) Noël played Hesketh-Baggott, head of an employment agency for gentlemen's gentlemen. Foster (John Gielgud, centre) has just left the taxing employ of Phileas Fogg, and Passepartout (Cantinflas, right) has hopes of taking his place.*

The premiere of Around the World—Marlene Dietrich, Noël, and David and Hjordis Niven.

Hesketh-Baggott raises the famous Coward forefinger as he admonishes Foster to never underestimate "the efficacy of prayer."

and sweetmeats, is a film like any other, only twice as long as most . . . the shots of trains and boats seem endless."

The film, nonetheless, did win the Academy Award for Best Picture for its year as well as several other craft awards.

* * * *

Asked to compare his new career of film actor with stage acting: "I think it's very, very valuable to have been a theatre actor, because of a sense of timing. But I find it terribly tedious making movies. For one reason only—the rest of it I enjoy very much, but the tedious thing is that you play a scene for the first time and the entire staff—convulsions! So then you do it another time for the sound, and then you do it again because the lighting hasn't been quite right, or *something's* gone wrong, and by the time you get to the actual take, they're all going about yawning and looking away, and wishing they weren't there. *That* is not encouraging for light comedy. *That's* what I don't like about filming."

AROUND THE WORLD IN EIGHTY DAYS (1956)

CREW
United Artists

Producer	Michael Todd
Director	Michael Anderson
Screenplay	James Poe, John Farrow and S. J. Perelman (Based on the novel by Jules Verne)
Photography	Lionel Lindon
Music	Victor Young
Titles	Saul Bass
Associate Producer	William Cameron Menzies

Narrator	Edward R. Murrow
CAST	
Phileas Fogg	David Niven
Passepartout	Cantinflas

With: Ronald Adam, Charles Boyer, Joe E. Brown, Martine Carol, John Carradine, Charles Coburn, Ronald Colman, Melville Cooper, Noël Coward, Finlay Currie, Reginald Denny, Andy Devine, Marlene Dietrich, Luis Dominguin, Fernandel, Walter Fitzgerald, John Gielgud, Hermione Gingold, José Greco, Cedric Hardwicke, Trevor Howard, Glynis Johns, Buster Keaton, Evelyn Keyes, Beatrice Lillie, Peter Lorre, Edmund Lowe, Shirley MacLaine, A. E. Matthews, Mike Mazurki, Tim McCoy, Victor McLaglen, John Mills, Alan Mowbray, Robert Morley, Robert Newton, Jack Oakie, George Raft, Gilbert Roland, Cesar Romero, Frank Sinatra, Red Skelton, Ronald Squire, Basil Sidney, Harcourt Williams.

STORY

Phileas Fogg, a very upright and rather humourless London clubman in Victorian England, is wagered by his fellow members that he cannot circumnavigate the globe in less than eighty days. He accepts the challenge and sets off, accompanied by his valet, Passepartout. After a series of varied adventures—including a few that were in Jules Verne's original story—he wins his bet and, in this case, the inevitable girl.

* * * *

Noël was sufficiently pleased with his showing in Todd's film that he needed little persuading to take on his next cameo in 1959.

"Carol Reed has asked me to play with Alec Guinness and Ralph Richardson in Graham Greene's *Our Man in Havana*. It's a good script and a very funny though small part. I think I shall do it. It means a few days location in Havana in April and about three weeks in London in June and July. All of which fits. We shall wait and see if the concessions and money are satisfactory." He added: "I suppose I shall spend most of my time dashing up side streets hotly pursued by Mr. Castro's wild friends." In fact, he did not.

Greene described Hawthorne as "tall and elegant, in his stone-coloured tropical suit, and wearing an exclusive tie, he carried with him the breath of beaches and the leathery smell of a good club; you expected to hear him say, 'The ambassador will see you in a minute.'"

Apparently everything was satisfactory and Noël took the part of Hawthorne (Agent 59200), a pompous and incompetent man from M.I.5, who arrives to "run" Wormold (Alec Guinness), the vacuum cleaner salesman he appoints as his agent in Havana. The scene where Hawthorne attempts to brief Wormold in the men's room of Sloppy Joe's bar so that the sound of running water will obscure their conversation is a classic of screen comedy.

Noël had every reason to suppose that Guinness would dominate the film. In the previous decade he had virtually owned British film comedy with such films as *Kind Hearts and Coronets, The Lavender Hill Mob, The Man in the White Suit, The Ladykillers* and many others. Nor was it his fault that he didn't add *Our Man* to his list.

In a series of letters to Noël after Noël had shot his scenes and departed, Guinness charts the progress of the project:

CAPRI – HAVANA APRIL 26TH 1959
Two or three nights ago I saw the first batch of rushes, including your street walking and Sloppy Joe's. In my opinion they were superb. Very funny, very excellent and they look marvellous. Carol's a clever old thing—what comes on the screen has such authority and decision and meaning. You look marvellous and the contrast between you and the Cubans create an effect of great brilliance without losing in any way reality.

Ernie Kovacs is VERY sweet and good natured but I think we are ALL prepared to brain him. The jokes are endless and ceaseless and exhausting to a degree. I'd far rather act with Renée Houston or appear in a chorus line. Between every take it's the gaiety or some gag he's thought up for his bloody TV show—AND he's a little fluffy on the lines. But good, I know. I've become so SQUARE in his eyes I'm positively CUBIC.

The girl (Jo Morrow) is still full of "Hi!" and "Get you!" and "Daddy-O!" and loud and bouncy but she has been told by Carol to calm down. I BELIEVE he's told her I'm too old for all that carry on. But I must say she performs well.

Burl Ives arrived last night, together with wife, guitar and personal press agent! He seems a dear—I'm sure he is—and v. good—but I KNOW he's going to sing to me when we have a quiet moment in the broiling sun.

DEC. 11 1959
It's funny how one is NEVER jealous of good actors—not in the remotest bit jealous of the huge and gay success you will make in it, but REJOICE in it.

But I shall be spitting fire if they think dear old Burl is good.

JAN. 5 1960
Most of the press were pretty beastly to me—and to the film, if it comes to that . . . I WAS dull in it—in spite of the kind things you say. I'm in a rather "I-told-you-so mood." I DID keep telling Carol I ought to have characterised it more as a shopman, perhaps with a squint, a wall eye, buck teeth and a mop of ginger hair and a Manchester accent. I don't feel bitter about it, though I knew perfectly well what was happening while doing it and I can't possibly blame Carol now that he is taking the rap as well as me. In fact I don't even blame him in my heart of hearts. In spite of weaknesses, I think it a good film—and thanks to you, Ralph and Ernie Kovacs, an entertaining one.

FEB. 4 1960
I'm told we are a big success in N.Y. and that the notices have been appreciably better and, of course, a triumph for you. I'm rather puzzled that Ernie Kovacs hasn't been appreciated more.

With the reviews in Noël himself could write: "I have had rave notices for my performance . . . The *Daily Mail* carried a screaming headline and stated that I had 'stolen the picture' from Alec Guinness. It then went on to insult Alec and the rest of the cast and abuse Carol Reed. Delighted as I am to have made such a spectacular success in what is after all a minor part, my pleasure is tempered with irritation at being used as a flail against my fellow artists. This is not noble modesty on my part. I *am* very good, the picture *is* slow in parts and Alec *is* dull at moments."

Peter John Dyer summed up a general view: "The main weakness is the absence of economic, expressive cutting and visual flow. As a result . . . stretches of dialogue become tedious to watch; and the essential awareness of the writer's shifting tensions yields disappointingly to the easier mannerisms of any conventional comedy-thriller."

The *New York Times:* "It is not until the delightfully crocky Noël Coward, lips pursed primly and umbrella cocked upon his arm had bullied a timid Mr. Guinness into the washroom of a famous bar and ordained him a spy for the British Secret Service that you realise a comedy is under way. Mr. Coward is beautifully brazen as a bumbling bureaucrat."

C. A. Lejeune was duly admiring of the professionalism on display. Noël, she felt, was "as inconspicuous as a hippopotamus in a tank of goldfish . . . a practised showman, he plays him with all his skills precisely as required." She was not, however, about to subscribe to the film stealing theory. "It is as stupid to say he steals the film as to claim that the man with the loudest laugh is the life and soul of the party."

The whole enterprise was hardly helped by being shot just weeks after Castro's take-over of the country—a happenstance which necessitated an opening caption stating that the events took place *before* the revolution. Filming was interrupted by the principals being summoned to meet the General, only to be left in ante rooms from which they could see Castro and his minions, wreathed in cigar smoke and engaged in angry conversation. One by one the filmmakers tired of the game and left. Guinness has the memory of Noël mouthing "Manana" to a lackey as he took his own leave.

OUR MAN IN HAVANA (1959)

CREW
Columbia Pictures
Producer/Director   Carol Reed
Screenplay from his
   original novel   Graham Greene
Photography   Oswald Morris
Editor   Bert Bates
Art Director   John Box

CAST
Jim Wormold   Alec Guinness
Dr. Hasselbacher   Burl Ives
Beatrice Stevens   Maureen O'Hara
Captain Segura   Ernie Kovacs
Hawthorne   Noël Coward

Raymond Huntley, Noël (Hawthorne), and Ralph Richardson ponder the impenetrable doings of their Man in Havana.

"C"	Ralph Richardson
Milly Wormold	Jo Morrow
Carter	Paul Rogers
Engineer Sifuentes	Gregoire Aslan
Lopez	José Prieto
Rudy	Timothy Bateson
MacDougal	Duncan Macrae
Navy Officer	Maurice Denham
Army Officer	Raymond Huntley
Professor Sanchez	Ferdy Mayne
Stripper	Yvonne Buckingham
Teresa	Maxine Audley
Dr. Braun	Karel Stepanek
Waiter	John Le Mesurier
Svenson	Gerik Schielderup
Beautiful Woman	Elizabeth Welch

STORY

Wormold is a retiring middle-aged man eking out a living selling vacuum cleaners in Batista's Cuba and trying to raise a teenage daughter, Millie. His idea of a good time is a drink and a chat with his German friend, Hasselbacher. One day he is visited by Hawthorne, a man from M.I.5, who proceeds to recruit him as "our man in Havana." Though reluctant at first, Wormold finds the money irresistible—"tax free," as Hawthorne reminds him. Not knowing how to set up a spy network, he invents "agents" and, to provide his London lords and masters with material, sends them enlarged copies of his various vacuum cleaners, which he claims are hideous new weapons under construction. M.I.5 accepts his story but events get out of hand when so does the "opposition." Hasselbacher is murdered—at which point the Wormold turns. The mild-mannered man ends up shooting an enemy agent and being deported to face his bosses, who can think of nothing better to protect their own reputations than to promote him.

* * * *

There was to be a second film in that year (1959) even before *Our Man* was released. In his *Diary* for November 22: "I am leaving for London today and start shooting the film *Surprise Package* tomorrow. It's a good part and they're paying me £35,000 and all expenses! . . . I read [the script] in an hour, and said 'Yes.' I would have said 'Yes' even if it had been in Sanskrit. Actually, it's very funny and well written." His ready agreement was due, at least in part, to the depleted state of his bank balance. Film acting for the next few years would remedy that and provide him with more income than he was deriving from his more conventional sources. These two films alone covered the cost of the house he had just bought in Switzerland.

A week later he could look back on a *fait accompli*. "Well, I've had an exhausting week but very satisfactory. I think I am going to be good in the picture. It's a very good part [Noël plays a king in exile, 'Pavel the Serene'] . . . Yul is a dear to work with, so is Mitzi Gaynor, and Stanley Donen is a really excellent director, gentle, thorough and patient. There is much less tension working with him than with Carol. Actually, I am enjoying doing it very much."

While his professional antennae were invariably sensitive to his own performance, Noël's desire to have the vehicle that was showcasing it shine frequently clouded his judgement. By this time Donen had been involved in many charming and successful films—*On the Town* (1949) and *Singin' in the Rain* (1952) with Gene Kelly, *Seven Brides for Seven Brothers* (1954) and *Funny Face* (1956) among them—but it seemed that when the music stopped, his touch wavered. Perhaps sensing that, he introduced a last minute musical number into *Surprise Package*.

Noël records: "All my principal scenes are now done, including a musical sequence in which I do a cheerful little number with Mitzi Gaynor. This was given to me on Wednesday morning at eleven o'clock. I learnt it and it was recorded and in the can by twelve o'clock. Everyone was very surprised but it really wasn't very difficult. The next day I mouthed it in the scene. I have never done this synchronisation before, but it was all right. I've enjoyed making this picture and have felt relaxed in front of the camera for the first time in my sporadic film experience."

He was being kind about the "cheerful little number," a hastily-contrived title song and far from being one of Sammy Cahn and Jimmy Van Heusen's best. Wisely, Noël never subsequently recorded it.

Playing with Yul Brynner completed a personal circle for Noël. Some years before he had been invited by Rodgers and Hammerstein to play the King in their forthcoming stage musical, *The King and I*. At Gertrude Lawrence's personal request they had agreed to adapt the film *Anna and the King of Siam* as a starring vehicle for her and felt that Noël would be a perfect partner. Much as he would have enjoyed playing opposite his beloved Gertie again, his dislike of long runs—and this was clearly likely to be a show that *would* run—he refused the part but recommended his two old friends to audition a young gypsy singer he'd heard play at a number of recent New York parties. The singer, of course, was the young Yul Brynner and the part began and eventually became his career.

Surprise Package was part of Brynner's attempt to diversify. Over the years he had limited success with dramatic parts but light comedy was not his forte. Even Noël was forced to admit this when he attended a sneak preview of the film in March 1960: "It is a funny picture, injured considerably by Yul's inaudibility and helped very much by me. Mitzi Gaynor charming. It will probably be a success but I am not dead sure. I think I'm fairly certain to be because my part is very funnily written and I do it very well."

Six months later when the film opened: "I have had rave notices and several headlines saying I 'steal' the picture from Yul. This, of course, is true but it is petty larceny."

The critics—most of whom wrote the film off—nevertheless considered it "another jewel in Coward's crown" (Dick Richards, *Daily Mirror*). "Noël Coward, of all incredible people, plays the exiled King whose hobby is collecting full grown nymphets with the air of an aging high

A publicity still for Stanley Donen's Surprise Package *(1960) in which Noël played King Pavel II opposite Yul Brynner. "I have had rave notices . . . saying I 'steal' the picture from Yul. This, of course, is true but it is petty larceny."*

priest of Tibet." "If it [his part] wasn't written by Noël Coward . . . it's the best imitation of him to date" (*Evening Standard*). The "picture stealer supreme" (*The Tatler*) . . . "with the least of effort . . . a song at the piano and a bit of jive is easily able to do to Brynner what he did to Guinness in *Our Man in Havana*—suggest that he is the superior star" (*Evening News*).

Harold Convy in the *Daily Sketch* agreed that Noël "blitzes Yul Brynner off the screen . . . with a casual variety of suave smiles and a sardonic lift of the eyebrows . . . Coward the actor is becoming the most brilliant, most formidable scene stealer in the business." Convy then went on to pinpoint the element that was essential to that success: "All his film roles so far are a mere extension of his personality."

SURPRISE PACKAGE (1960)

CREW
Columbia Pictures

Producer	Stanley Donen
Director	Stanley Donen
Screenplay	Harry Kurnitz
	(From the novel by Art Buchwald)
Photography	Christopher Challis
Titles	Maurice Binder

CAST

Nico March	Yul Brynner
King Pavel II	Noël Coward
Gaby Rogers	Mitzi Gaynor
Police Chief	Eric Pohlmann
Dr. Panze	George Coulouris

With: Warren Mitchell, Bill Nagy, Guy Déghy, Lydon Brook

STORY
An American gangster is deported to the same Mediterranean island as an exiled European king, whose crown gets stolen.

*   *   *   *

There was rather less to enjoy about his next assignment—*Paris When It Sizzles* in 1962.

Every now and then Hollywood sees the kind of film its studio system is totally ill-equipped to make and decides to remake it. When the original is a slight piece of gallic whimsy, the results are usually disastrous, and so it proved when Paramount decided to remake *La Fête à Henriette* as *Paris When It Sizzles*. The title should have been a clue.

On paper the project looked promising. Director Richard Quine had a good comedy pedigree—*The Solid Gold Cadillac* (1956) and *Bell, Book and*

Candle (1958); writer George Axelrod was the author of *The Seven Year Itch* (1955); and the two stars—William Holden and Audrey Hepburn—both had enviable box office reputations. A few years earlier they had costarred in the successful Billy Wilder film, *Sabrina* (1954). Despite the quality of the ingredients, however, the *soufflé* failed to rise.

In September 1962 Noël notes that he will be going to Paris for three days: "George Axelrod rang me up and asked me to play a small but effective part in the movie he is doing with Audrey Hepburn and Bill Holden. He hurried the script to me and the scene is effective although tiny, but I am being paid $10,000 and all luxe expenses, and so I said yes, I think it will be rather fun. The part is that of a Hungarian movie producer (? Alex Korda) dressed in a Roman toga at a fancy dress party. I shall enjoy doing the accent."

During shooting one scene turned into two. We first meet Noël's character (Alexander Meyerheim) lying by the pool at the Eden Roc in Cap d'Antibes and then later—far too much later—at the Roman party. For the stretches in between the two stars try their best to inject life into a story in which each of them is required to play cliché fictional parts, rather than be the two film star personalities audiences came to see.

There is a sad irony in Noël's opening scene. Told by a rival producer that his writer (Richard Benson) failed to complete his last picture because of his drinking problem, Meyerheim says optimistically: "Richard assures me that, for all practical purposes, he is on the wagon." As it turned out shooting on *Paris* was held up when William Holden—well advanced with his own battle with alcohol that would eventually kill him—was involved in a car accident.

At the time Noël appeared to notice few of the production's stresses and strains. Not for the first time—having committed himself to a project—he was inclined to see what he wanted to see. In his *Diary* for October lst he notes:

In Paris When It Sizzles *Alexander Meyerheim—or could it be Korda? (Noël)—is a film producer whose parties are as lavish as his productions. Except, unfortunately, this film in which he happens to be appearing.*

My four days' sojourn in Paris was really an unqualified success . . . George A. said they did *not* want me to play the part with an accent but to be super Noël Coward. This rather threw me; however, I decided to use irrepressible laughter as the basis of my performance and just wing it on that one technical trick. It worked like a charm and I have never had such a fuss made. Dick Quine, the director, and a sweet man, carried on alarming. Audrey H., unquestionably the nicest and most talented girl in the business, deluged me with praise and roses. Bill Holden, *off* the bottle and looking fifteen years younger, charming to work with . . . The set; the Eiffel Tower Restaurant, was marvellous, but the heat of the lights appalling. I worked for three days dressed in a white and gold satin tunic, laced up gold boots, a magnificent scarlet, gold-fringed cloak, and a wreath of gilt leaves on my head. George showed me about half the picture—rough-cut; it really is very funny and Audrey and Bill are enchanting. So is Tony Curtis and so, apparently, am I. So that is a neat little job done. I did my big speech in two takes without fluffing once, and I must say I thoroughly enjoyed myself.

The critics, however—who were not being paid $10,000—found the prospect less enchanting. The *New York Times* spoke for most of them: "*Paris When It Sizzles* is a rock-hard chestnut that is hard to savor or swallow."

PARIS WHEN IT SIZZLES (1963)

CREW
Paramount Pictures
Producer/Director — Richard Quine
Screenplay — George Axelrod
(Based on *La Fête à Henriette* by Julien Duvalier and Henri Jeason)
Photography — Charles Lang Jr.
Music — Nelson Riddle
Editor — Archie Marsher

CAST
Richard Benson — William Holden
Gabrielle Simpson — Audrey Hepburn
Phillipe/Maurice — Tony Curtis
Inspector Gillet — Gregoire Aslan
Alexander Mayerheim — Noël Coward
Party Guests — Raymond Bussières, Marlene Dietrich, Fred Astaire, Frank Sinatra, Mel Ferrer

STORY
A fading screenwriter working on a script in Paris falls in love with his temporary secretary. He tries out several of his plot ideas with the two of them as the various heroes, heroines and villains.

* * * *

In 1965 Noël was reunited for the first time with Laurence Olivier since *Private Lives* (1930)—even though they didn't actually share a scene together. Olivier played the deadpan detective searching for the missing daughter of an American girl in London in Otto Preminger's *Bunny Lake Is Missing*. Cheerfully putting aside his hair piece, Noël played Wilson, the seedy old boarding house keeper for rather more than the part was worth. "The role amused me. But I don't think I raise my aristocratic nose at the thought of a few thousand dollars, too!"

So disreputable was the character that Noël remarked: "You'd really think I was a modern young actor on his way to rehearsal." Describing the part to a friend, he said: "I play an elderly, drunk, queer masochist and I am in no mood for any wisecracks about typecasting." He carried a tiny chihuahua "crooked in my arm. It just lies there comatose but quivering. I can't stand things that quiver . . . It only has one piece of action . . . it had to wave, but it couldn't do it. I said to it, 'You will never make another Lassie.'"

Carol Lynley has a visit from Wilson (Noël) and a canine companion.

He confided to his *Diary:* "I found Otto Preminger an excellent director and I think I am good in it." Indeed he was but the film itself—Preminger's half-hearted would-be-*Laura*-revisited story was a thing of shreds badly in need of patching. The character of Horatio Wilson ("poet, playwright and dropper of alcoholic bricks") looks like Preminger's attempt to do a Hitchcock. How can someone of Coward's eminence be playing a character that isn't significant in the plot? We see him tantalisingly twice and he turns out to have nothing whatsoever to do with the story. So unless the director was obliged to leave material on the cutting room floor—in which case we should certainly have heard about it from Noël!—the role was essentially one of red herring. A point picked up by the *New York Times* (among others), which considered it "a specious and unconvincing picture."

Preminger was apparently nonplussed by the nostalgic shorthand between his two stars who reminisced about events of thirty years previously. At the end of filming Noël suggested to the director that they really should do a play together sometime—which could easily be a Cowardesque way of saying that he didn't consider Preminger's earlier TV efforts with *Tonight at 8:30* to be worth the name.

BUNNY LAKE IS MISSING (1965)

CREW
Columbia Pictures
Producer/Director   Otto Preminger
Screenplay   John and Penelope Mortimer
                         (From a novel by Evelyn Piper)
Photography   Denys Coop
Titles   Saul Bass

CAST
Superintendent Newhouse Laurence Olivier
"Mrs." Ann Lake   Carol Lynley
Steven Lake   Keir Dullea
Sgt. Andrews   Clive Revill
Ada Ford   Martita Hunt
Elvira Smollett   Anna Massey
Horatio Wilson   Noël Coward
Doll Repairer   Finlay Currie
Cook   Lucie Mannheim
With: Adrienne Corri

STORY
Mrs. Lake arrives in London with her small illegitimate daughter, Bunny. She has come to join her journalist brother, Steven, with whom she has always been close. While she moves into her new flat, she leaves Bunny at the day school. Returning to pick her up, she finds the child is missing and no one remembers seeing her. The police investigate and the lack of evidence

seems to point to Bunny being a figment of her imagination. It transpires that Steven, fixated on his sister, has abducted the little girl, so that he can have his sister to himself once again.

* * * *

Though not a film *per se*, in 1967 Noël made "a brisk trip to New York to play Caesar in Dick Rodgers' *Androcles and the Lion* for a television (musical) special. Joe Layton directed it very well and everyone was extremely nice, but I didn't enjoy any of it. I hate television anyway. It has all the nervous pressure of a first night with none of the response. However," he concluded, "I was apparently very good."

Variety was a little more qualified in its praise: "Noël Coward, absent too long from American home screens, played Caesar with the blithest possible spirit. His rapid speech, however, was not always captured by the mikes."

Noël sang two numbers, "The Emperor's Thumb" and "Don't Be Afraid of an Animal" (a duet with Norman Wisdom).

ANDROCLES AND THE LION (1967)

CREW
Director	Joe Layton
Book by	Peter Stone (based on the play by George Bernard Shaw)
Music and Lyrics	Richard Rodgers

CAST
Caesar	Noël Coward
Androcles	Norman Wisdom
Lion	Geoffrey Holder
Megaera	Patricia Routledge
Captain	John Cullum
Lavinia	Inge Swenson
Lentulus	Brian Bedford
Metellus	Clifford Davis
Ferrovius	Ed Ames
Pintho	William Redfield
Manager of Gladiators	Kurt Kaznar
Roman Centurion	George Matthews
Keeper of the Lions	Bill Hickey
Retiarius and Lion	Bill Star
Secutor and Lion	George Reeder
Lion	Steve Bookvar

* * * *

In his career as a film actor Noël worked with some formidable and proven talents. Unfortunately, he rarely managed to work with them when they were living up to their reputations. Carol Reed, Stanley Donen, Richard Quine, Otto Preminger—he had encountered all of them on an off day rather than

in their decline—but he was not to appear in their more lasting work. His own performance usually managed to shine like a good deed in if not a naughty then at least a boring world. The same thing was to happen in 1968, when he worked with Joseph Losey on *Boom*.

Losey had been a minor Hollywood director who found himself swept up in the Senator Joe McCarthy net of alleged Communists and fellow travellers. Once on the "black list," he had decamped—like so many others—for the United Kingdom where, after a period as a "shadow" director with someone else receiving the screen credit, he emerged as one of the most significant of the British cinema's post-war directors.

Films such as *The Servant* (1963) and *Accident* (1967) had dealt with people in precarious emotional states. As his cult status grew, affectation was never far away and with *Boom* he crossed the line. To be fair, he was helped immensely by one of Tennessee Williams's more pretentious screenplays, drawn from a little-regarded early play that might better have remained *un*regarded.

Noël plays the Witch of Capri—a female character in the original play—and the film was shot in Sardinia, a location that appealed to the hedonist in Noël. He found the island "in the first place most beautiful and bathed in lovely sunshine all the time . . . everyone concerned with the picture was charming and friendly. I love Liz Taylor and found her a million per cent professional and wonderful to work with. Richard, of course, was sweet and the director, Joe Losey, a dear man. I had a bit of trouble with Tennessee's curiously phrased dialogue, but apart from that, everything was halcyon. Acting for the movies in such very pleasant circumstances is really great fun."

The "bit of trouble" he alluded to was the progression of the memory failure he had first experienced during the stage run of *Suite in Three Keys* (1966), when he had had trouble with the lines that he had written himself. Shortly before starting *Boom* it had recurred during the taping of *Androcles and the Lion*. It seems to have been a side effect of the arteriosclerosis that was progressively affecting him and which he refused to take seriously. Nonetheless, after *Suite* even he realised that he could no longer act on stage. For Noël, who had always prided himself on his ability to learn prodigious amounts of dialogue at great speed and arrive word perfect, this was a bitter experience and the likelihood is that he felt rather less happy about film acting, once it became the only alternative left to him. However, the path he trod was one shared by some eminent company. In their later years both Laurence Olivier and John Gielgud made considerable and profitable new careers as film "character" actors.

In December 1967 Noël could record: "Saw a rough cut of *Goforth* [the film's working title]. I'm not sure it will storm the world, but I'm quite good and look all right."

In point of fact, it turned out to be one of Noël's best screen performances from the moment he entered carried on the shoulders of one of Mrs. Goforth's servants. The character is also close to the waspish, articulate urbanity people had come to expect of his public persona.

While the critics generally dismissed the film for what it was, an overblown confection, most of them enjoyed the spectacle of Noël enjoying himself. "A terrifying cameo," said Richard Roud in the *Guardian*, "Noël Coward drops in to hoot with hollow mirth."

BOOM (1968)

CREW
Universal Pictures
Producers	John Heyman/Norman Priggen
Director	Joseph Losey
Screenplay	Tennessee Williams from his play
	The Milk Train Doesn't Stop Here Any More
	and short story *Man Bring This Up Road*
Photography	Douglas Slocombe
Music	John Barry
Production Design	Richard Macdonald

CAST
Mrs. Flora Goforth	Elizabeth Taylor
Christopher Flanders	Richard Burton
(The Angel of Death)	
The Witch of Capri	Noël Coward

"Darling, are we quite sure about the hat?" Elizabeth Taylor seems eager to persuade Noël (the Witch of Capri).

Blackie	Joanna Shimkus
Rudy	Michael Dunn
Dr. Lullo	Romolo Valli
Etti	Fernando Piazza
Simonetta	Veronica Wells
Manicurist	Claudye Ettori
Photographer	Gens Bloch
Journalist	Howard Taylor
Villager	Franco Pesce

STORY

Mrs. Goforth is a dying millionairess living in isolated splendour on an inaccessible rocky Mediterranean island. A wandering poet and artist finds his way there and she plans to take him as her last lover. Her one local friend—a society gossip known as the Witch of Capri—warns her that the young man, Christopher Flanders, has gained the reputation of being the "Angel of Death," due to the fact that he seems to have a habit of arriving uninvited in households where someone is about to die. By the time Flora Goforth joins the list, there has been a great deal of portentous talk about the meaning of life and death and endless shots of the sea beating itself on the rocks—hence the film's title.

* * * *

There was a particular personal pleasure to Noël's next—and, as it turned out, his last—film part. The director was Peter Collinson, "the little Actors' Orphanage boy whom I saved from expulsion by giving him a brisk heart-to-heart talk on a garden seat," a reference to his long lasting involvement with that particular charity, which he had inherited from his stage mentor, Sir Gerald du Maurier, in 1934 and was to continue until 1956.

There was no symbolism or pretension about *The Italian Job*. It was a good old-fashioned "caper" film in which a bunch of small time crooks, masterminded from prison by Mr. Bridger (Noël), the middle class English equivalent of a Mafia gang boss, plan and pull off a bullion raid using a fleet of Minis. Much of the filming was done in Dublin "and great fun it was," Noël wrote in early September 1968.

> There are still a few interiors to be done here (London) at Isleworth. Michael Caine is a darling to work with, swift, efficient and with a comforting sense of humour. It's incredible to think, listening to his light, charming speaking voice, that he started life as a Cockney barrow-boy in Whitechapel. We had a lovely time working together and I enjoyed every scene I played with him. Peter reigned benevolently over us with his heart glinting in the sunlight. It will be, I think, a good picture. Altogether a very satisfying experience.
>
> We came back yesterday on a chartered plane, which always frightens the shit out of me. However, we landed gracefully and no wings fell off.

Asked his thoughts on playing a crook, he thought for a moment: "Artists and criminals have something in common, I suppose. After all, they mingle at lot."

Reviews were generally favourable with only the *New York Times* offering a slightly edgy note. The review of October 6, 1969, offered the thought that "the movie exploits him in various unpleasant ways, including décor. His prison cell is decorated with pictures of the Royal Family that in real life has never seen fit to knight him." But the calendar caught up with their critic. In the New Year's Honours List for 1970 that was taken care of.

This time Noël's prognostication proved correct. *The Italian Job* was a commercial success but the review that must have pleased Noël more than any other was Michael Caine's verdict: "Playing with Noël," he told an interviewer, "is a lot like working with God."

THE ITALIAN JOB (1969)

CREW
Paramount Pictures

Producer	Michael Deeley
Director	Peter Collinson
Screenplay	Troy Kennedy Martin
Photography	Douglas Slocombe
Music	Quincy Jones

CAST:

Charlie Croker	Michael Caine
Mr. Bridger	Noël Coward
Prof. Peach	Benny Hill
Mafia Boss (Altabarie)	Raf Vallone
Camp. Freddie	Tony Beckley
Beckerman	Rosanno Brazzi
Lorna	Maggie Blye
Miss Peach	Irene Handl
Prison Governor	John Le Mesurier
Birkinshaw	Fred Emney
Keats	Graham Payn

STORY

From his lavishly-appointed prison cell Mr. Bridger—a crime lord in temporary residence—master-minds "the Italian job," an attempt to hijack £4 million in gold bullion the Chinese are paying the Fiat company to build a car factory in Italy. He appoints Charlie Croker and an assorted band of small time crooks to tamper with the traffic computer in Turin while the city is distracted with an international football match. They get away with the gold using a fleet of British Minis to outwit the local police and Mafia pursuit and *almost* win the day for the old country.

* * * *

"For what we are about to receive . . . " Mr. Bridger dines alone during The Italian Job.

There was to be a coda to the career of Noël Coward, Actor.

Looking around for a musical blockbuster to follow his earlier *West Side Story* (1961) and *The Sound of Music* (1965), director Robert Wise hit upon the idea of a film biography of Gertrude Lawrence. Gertie would be played by Julie Andrews, then at the height of her reputation after *The Sound of Music* (in which she had starred for Wise) and *Mary Poppins* (1964), for which she had won the Oscar.

There are always problems in casting the "lives" of near contemporaries, since so many of the characters are still around to have their say. No such concerns of possible libel or slander exist with regard to the deceased. The filmmakers could, so to speak, take liberties with Gertie—but what about Noël?

Out of common sense and courtesy the producers showed him the script (by William Fairchild). He let it go with only one recorded comment. Handing it back to the nervous writer, he observed: "Dear boy, there are too many 'Dear boys,' in those lines, dear boy."

Strictly speaking, this was to be the second time Noël would be depicted on screen—though the first using his own name. In the Moss Hart–George S. Kaufman play *The Man Who Came to Dinner* there was a Cowardesque character, Beverly Carlton, for whom Cole Porter wrote a "Noël Coward-type song" ("What Am I to Do?"). When the play was filmed in 1941 the character—now for some reason called Beverly Garland—was played by Reginald Gardiner.

Beatrice Lillie—Gertie's early partner in the 1920s *Charlot Revues* and an old friend of both Noël and Gertie—proved more difficult, though not in a predictable way. Now exhibiting more advanced signs of the memory problems she had suffered four years earlier, when appearing in *High Spirits* (the musical version of *Blithe Spirit*), she declared herself totally in favour of the film. "And, of course, darling—I shall play myself!" Sensing that directing an undirectable woman of seventy to play a girl in her twenties, Wise wisely cut the character entirely, substituting Billie Carlton, one of his own invention.

He was obliged to do this if he was to stage one of the key scenes in Noël's early career in which Noël—introduced in real life by Bea Lillie—auditions for Charlot. In the film, as in real life, he performs what he considered to be his own first song—"Forbidden Fruit." In the film—as in real life—Charlot hates both it and him and chastises the Lillie character for wasting his time on someone with so little talent. In the film—as in real life—he was rapidly to revise that verdict.

Star! turned out to be an overlong and amiable film lacking completely the spark that Wise had brought to his earlier work. Perhaps the subject was intractable for a commercial film of the period. Gertrude Lawrence was not a woman made of peaches and cream, sweetness and light—that was what made her so fascinating. Among other things, her friends knew her to be a spendthrift, amoral, talented and charming bitch goddess. Julie Andrews she was not and, despite her skill with many of the musical numbers, Andrews is clearly uncomfortable playing the hoyden aspects of Lawrence's character. Noël—who was fond of her—praised parts of her performance, offering only the caveat that she "lacked Gertie's gamine quality." Privately, he had believed from the start of the project that "Gertie's life wasn't the stuff of dreams."

For the screen "Noël" he had mostly praise. He was played by his own godson, Daniel Massey, a young actor who had appeared (as an even younger actor) as Noël's son in *In Which We Serve*. Brushing aside the fact that Massey was the better looking of the two, Noël focused beadily on his faults. "He made one grave tactical error," he told an interviewer with straight face. "He *sang* better!" Then for once he couldn't help smiling toothily at his own joke.

The critics were less than enthusiastic, although many of them clearly wanted to like the film. The *New York Times* summed up its review by concluding: "People who liked Gertrude Lawrence had better stick with their record collections and memories."

STAR! (1968)

CREW
Twentieth Century Fox

Producer	Saul Chaplin
Director	Robert Wise
Screenplay	William Fairchild
Photography	Ernest Laszlo
Choreography	Michael Kidd
Title Song	Sammy Cahn and Jimmy Van Heusen

CAST

Gertrude Lawrence	Julie Andrews
Noël Coward	Daniel Massey
Richard Aldrich	Richard Crenna
Sir Anthony Spencer	Michael Craig
Charles Fraser	Robert Reed
Arthur Lawrence	Bruce Forsyth
Rose	Beryl Reid
Lawrence's Daughter	Jenny Agutter

The film was subsequently and severely cut and re-released under the title— *Those Were The Happy Days*

*   *   *   *

As a film actor Noël was an early starter but a late developer. Part of this had to do with the many other activities that claimed his time and competed for his attention. Most of it was because he was essentially a man of the theatre.

"I'll always love the theatre a little better and I know why that is," he told an interviewer late in life. "It's the contact with an audience. I'd rather play a bad matinée at Hull—incidentally, I've never played a *good* matinée!—than do a movie, even though I enjoy doing movies." Not for the first time he was guilty of letting a good line obscure his true feeling, for by this time (1969) he was revelling in his latest role of archcriminal when it came to stealing films.

In a less flippant mood he was more revealing: "I learned, when I started doing movies, an enormous amount that helped me as an actor—the meticulousness . . . On the stage you can make a little fluff, give a merry laugh and get on with it. And nobody notices. In the movies, one wrong word and 'Cut!' And I *hate* that word 'Cut!' Another aspect that appealed to him was the immediacy of filming. Even in his beloved theatre he had a dislike of long runs and refused to appear for more than a few months, even in his own hits such as *Private Lives*. "The fascinating thing about filming is that each day you have something different to do. The boring part of the theatre is that you have to do the same thing eight times a week."

Apart from Griffith's early advice—subsequently repeated by Carol Reed—not to use so much "lip," he learned several other acting lessons from his screen appearances. *In Which We Serve* and his role as a reserved naval officer taught him to economise on the use of his hands and to depend more on facial expression. He also had to learn to adapt his vocal delivery: "I have to relearn once more not to pitch my voice to the back of the gallery . . . not to 'put in' expression . . . I still feel that acting for the 'silver screen' is fairly silly and infinitely difficult [This in an early interview]. But I expect that's because I'm inexperienced and don't do it very well." It would be 1960 and *Surprise Package* before he could admit that he felt comfortable in front of the camera for the first time.

Like all true film stars, he developed a strong sense of how he should be filmed to best advantage: "The whole secret of photographing this enchanting, heart-shaped face is to have a diagonal shadow falling across the forehead. A naval cap set at a rakish angle contrived this so cleverly in *In Which We Serve*. The effect was heavenly. I can't wear a naval cap in this film, but, dear boy," he advised the cameraman, "don't despair. In the close-ups all you need is the subtlest strand falling across the brilliant marble dome. And in those vast exteriors, when I pause for a moment's inspiration in dappled sunlight, arrange it so that an overhanging branch is waving above me, ever so casually."

There's a strong case for arguing that Noël would never have been a successful leading man in films, unless he had been playing one of his own bespoke parts. The abbreviated TV version suggests that he would have made an excellent Charles Condomine in *Blithe Spirit*; the pity is that CBS and Ford's myopia prevented us from having even that sort of record of perhaps his best later part—Garry Essendine in *Present Laughter*. Those are the "if only" roles.

Of the parts he did play only three can be considered "leads" and between them they underscore the essential dilemma Noël faced as a film actor.

In *The Scoundrel* he was required to play a version of the public image he had created by that time (1935) in the public mind. Seven years later in *In Which We Serve* he had to play against that image to achieve credibility as an "ordinary" man—a feat the critics generally agreed he managed to pull off. As it happened, this story of group heroism would have been hopelessly unbalanced by a "star" leading performance. By the time of *The Astonished Heart* (1950), cinema audiences were no longer prepared to accept him playing a part at variance with his public persona; they felt cheated.

In essence his problem was being "Noël Coward." It affected the perception of everything he did and it was only when he and those who employed him accepted that reality and used it that he emerged, late but successful, as Noël Coward: Character Actor, with each part a variation on that proven theme.

It's interesting, though fruitless, to speculate on what might have happened if that process of diversification had started earlier, but then the same is true of Noël's career as a whole.

Many people have made significant careers out of the parts Noël turned down over the years. Supposing he'd played Harry Lime, the part that eventually went to Orson Welles in *The Third Man* (1949); David Selznick wanted him to play opposite Cary Grant but at the time he was in the middle of a feud with Graham Greene. Suppose he'd played the Prince opposite Judy Holliday in the film version of Terence Rattigan's *The Sleeping Prince*, a project that was mooted in 1955? Olivier eventually played the part opposite Marilyn Monroe in the 1957 *The Prince and the Showgirl.* Suppose he'd played Colonel Nicholson, the role that won Alec Guinness the Oscar in David Lean's *The Bridge on the River Kwai* (1957)? ("What put me off was that everybody seemed to spend so much time under water.") Or Humbert Humbert in Stanley Kubrick's *Lolita* (1962)? ("At my time of life the film story would be logical if the twelve year old heroine was a sweet, little old lady.") The same year he turned down the part of Dr. No in his friend Ian Fleming's first James Bond film with the telegraphed reply: "No, no—a thousand times 'No!'" When he saw the finished film he found it "thoroughly enjoyable but, of course, idiotic. I'm glad I didn't play it."

All these parts and more were offered to him; anyone would have established him as a serious and bankable screen presence years before "Dad's Renaissance" of the mid-1960s dramatically marked up the Coward stock. But by this time his critics had finally got to him. He was probably too nervous to move so far from what he knew and give them such a sitting target. The insouciance was still there but it was surface deep. He should have started sooner.

His own thoughts on the subject are more revealing in his *Diary* than in the formal interview. In February 1956: "I feel the urge to make another movie and also to appear on the silver screen in a lighter mood than I have hitherto. In *The Scoundrel* I was drowned and spent a lot of time in the water; in *In Which We Serve* I was submerged in a tank for a large part of the picture, and in *The Astonished Heart* I was utterly miserable, soaked with rain and finally committed suicide. I would like to play a part in which I was cheerful throughout and bone dry. I feel also that from the vulgar financial point of view this ought to be a profitable idea and, what to me is most important, it could be fun to do."

By this time, of course, he had already appeared in Mike Todd's *Around the World in Eighty Days*, stayed bone dry and been cheerful throughout—particularly when he received so much for doing so little. For the last decade of his life his ears were always ready to prick up at the roar of the greasepaint, the smell of celluloid and the whisper of a pen signing a cheque.

Select Bibliography

Aldgate, Anthony, and Jeffrey Richards. *Britain Can Take It: The British Cinema in the Second World War.* Edinburgh: Edinburgh University Press, 1994.

Armes, Roy. *A Critical History of British Cinema.* Oxford: Oxford University Press, 1978.

Barr, Charles, ed. *All Our Yesterdays: 90 Years of British Cinema.* London: BFI Books, 1986.

Brownlow, Kevin. *David Lean: A Biography.* New York: St. Martin's Press, 1996.

Brunel, Adrian. *Nice Work: The Story of Thirty Years in British Film Production.* London: Forbes Robertson, 1949.

Coward, Noël. *Autobiography (consisting of Present Indicative, Future Indefinite and the uncompleted Past Conditional).* London: Methuen, 1986.

Durgnat, Raymond. *A Mirror for England: British Movies from Austerity to Affluence.* London: Faber and Faber, 1970.

Fairbanks, Douglas, Jr. *The Salad Days.* London: HarperCollins, 1988.

Fleming, Kate. *Celia Johnson.* London: Weidenfeld and Nicolson, 1991.

Gish, Lillian. *The Movies, Mr. Griffith and Me.* Englewood Cliffs, NJ: Prentice-Hall, 1969.

Maxford, Howard. *David Lean.* London: Batsford, 2000.

Neame, Ronald, with Barbara Roisman Cooper. *Straight from the Horse's Mouth.* Lanham, MD: Scarecrow, 2003.

Payn, Graham, with Barry Day. *My Life with Noël Coward.* New York: Applause Books, 1994.

Payn, Graham, and Sheridan Morley, ed. *The Noël Coward Diaries.* London: Weidenfeld and Nicolson, 1982.

Perry George. *The Great British Picture Show.* Boston: Little, Brown and Company, 1974.

Silver, Alain, and James Ursin. *David Lean and His Films.* London: Leslie Frewin, 1974.

Silverman, Stephen M. *David Lean.* New York: Harry N. Abrams, 1989.

Wapshott, Nicholas. *The Man Between: A Biography of Carol Reed.* London: Chatto and Windus, 1990.

Index

Titles follow the name in brackets in cases where Noël first knew someone as a commoner.
An italicised page number indicates a photograph.

About the Author

Barry Day is the author or editor of numerous books and plays with an emphasis on theatre—particularly musical theatre. In his twenty-plus years working with the Noël Coward estate, he has produced *Noël Coward: The Complete Lyrics*; *Collected Sketches and Parodies*; *Theatrical Companion to Coward, Updated Edition*; *A Life in Quotes*; and *The Unknown Noël: New Writing from the Coward Archive*, as well as concert versions of the Coward musicals *After the Ball* and *Pacific 1860*.

Day has edited literary "autobiographies" in the A Life . . . in His Own Words series, including those of Oscar Wilde, P. G. Wodehouse, and Dorothy Parker. He was part of the team that rebuilt Shakespeare's Globe playhouse on London's Bankside, and he wrote *This Wooden "O": Shakespeare's Globe Reborn*, the official account of that historic project. He is also the editor of *The Complete Lyrics of P. G. Wodehouse*, published in 2004 by Scarecrow Press.

Barry was awarded the O.B.E. in the Queen's Birthday Honours List in June 2004.